Rotkäppchen und andere Kindermärchen

Little Red Riding Hood and other Grimm Fairy Tales

[Bilingual Edition]

German – English

by Jacob and Wilhelm Grimm

Translated by Möwenstein

ISBN: 979-8-89513-208-1

Original text: *Little Red Riding Hood and other Grimm Fairy Tales* (1812)
by Jacob Grimm (1785-1863) and Wilhelm Grimm (1786-1859)

This bilingual edition—including translation, editorial revisions, formatting, and supplementary content—is produced and edited by Mowenstein Books LLC, with the original text faithfully reproduced from public-domain sources.

While every effort has been made to ensure accuracy, minor discrepancies may occur. Readers are encouraged to consult the original text for reference.

Cover Art: Inspired by *Hustling Sunlight* by Matthew Bakkom (www.hustlingsunlight.xyz)

Möwenstein Books™ is a trademark of and imprint published by Mowenstein Books LLC.

For permissions or inquiries:

Website: mowenstein.com
Email: copyright@mowenstein.com

Mowenstein Books LLC
DE, USA

Contents

Brüderchen und Schwesterchen

Little Brother and Little Sister

1.1 Brüderchen nahm sein Schwesterchen an der Hand und sprach:

Brother took his little sister by the hand and said:

1.2 »Seit die Mutter tot ist, haben wir keine gute Stunde mehr;

"We haven't had a good hour since our mother died;

1.3 die Stiefmutter schlägt uns alle Tage, und wenn wir zu ihr kommen, stößt sie uns mit den Füßen fort.

our stepmother beats us every day, and when we come to her, she pushes us away with her feet.

1.4 Die harten Brotkrusten, die übrig bleiben, sind unsere Speise, und dem Hündlein unter dem Tisch geht's besser:

The hard crusts of bread that are left over are our food, and the little dog under the table is better off:

1.5 dem wirft sie doch manchmal einen guten Bissen zu.

sometimes she throws it a good morsel.

Daß Gott erbarm, wenn das unsere Mutter wüßte! Komm, 1.6
God have mercy if our mother knew that! Come,

wir wollen miteinander in die weite Welt gehen.« 1.7
let's go out into the wide world together."

Sie gingen den ganzen Tag über Wiesen, Felder und Steine, und wenn es regnete, sprach das Schwesterchen: 1.8
They walked all day over meadows, fields and stones, and when it rained, the little sister said:

»Gott und unsere Herzen die weinen zusammen!« 1.9
"God and our hearts cry together!"

Abends kamen sie in einen großen Wald und wären so müde von Jammer, Hunger und dem langen Weg, daß sie sich in einen hohlen Baum setzten und einschliefen. 1.10
In the evening, they came to a large forest and were so tired from misery, hunger and the long journey that they sat down in a hollow tree and fell asleep.

Am anderen Morgen, als sie aufwachten, stand die Sonne schon hoch am Himmel und schien heiß in den Baum hinein. 2.1
The next morning, when they woke up, the sun was already high in the sky and shining hotly into the tree.

Da sprach das Brüderchen: 2.2
Then the little brother said,

»Schwesterchen, mich dürstet, wenn ich ein Brünnlein wüßte, ich ging und tränk einmal; 2.3
"Little sister, I'm thirsty, if I knew of a little fountain, I'd go and drink once;

2.4 ich mein, ich hörte eins rauschen.«

I think I heard the sound of one."

2.5 Brüderchen stand auf, nahm Schwesterchen an der Hand, und sie wollten das Brünnlein suchen.

Little brother got up, took little sister by the hand and they went to look for the fountain.

2.6 Die böse Stiefmutter aber war eine Hexe und hatte wohl gesehen, wie die beiden Kinder fortgegangen waren, war ihnen nachgeschlichen, heimlich, wie die Hexen schleichen, und hatte alle Brunnen im Walde verwünscht.

But the wicked stepmother was a witch and had seen the two children go away and had crept after them, secretly, as witches sneak, and had cursed all the wells in the forest.

2.7 Als sie nun ein Brünnlein fanden, das so glitzerig über die Steine sprang, wollte das Brüderchen daraus trinken, aber das Schwesterchen hörte wie es im Rauschen sprach:

When they found a little fountain that jumped so glitteringly over the stones, the little brother wanted to drink from it, but the little sister heard it murmur:

2.8 »Wer aus mir trinkt, wird ein Tiger;

"Whoever drinks from me will become a tiger;

2.9 wer aus mir trinkt, wird ein Tiger.«

whoever drinks from me will become a tiger."

2.10 Da rief das Schwesterchen:

Then the little sister called out:

2.11 »Ich bitte dich, Brüderchen, trink nicht, sonst wirst du ein wildes Tier und zerreißt mich.«

"Please don't drink, little brother, or you will become a wild animal and tear me apart."

3

Das Brüderchen trank nicht, ob es gleich so großen Durst hatte, und sprach,
2.12
The little brother did not drink, even though he was very thirsty, and said,

»Ich will warten bis zur nächsten Quelle.«
2.13
"I will wait until the next spring."

Als sie zum zweiten Brünnlein kamen, hörte das Schwesterchen, wie auch dieses sprach:
2.14
When they came to the second fountain, the little sister heard this one also say:

»Wer aus mir trinkt, wird ein Wolf:
2.15
"Whoever drinks from me will become a wolf:

wer aus mir trinkt, wird ein Wolf.«
2.16
whoever drinks from me will become a wolf."

Da rief das Schwesterchen:
2.17
Then the little sister cried,

»Brüderchen, ich bitte dich, trink nicht, sonst wirst du ein Wolf und frißt mich.«
2.18
"Brother, I beg you not to drink, or you will become a wolf and eat me."

Das Brüderchen trank nicht und sprach:
2.19
The little brother did not drink and said,

»Ich will warten, bis wir zur nächsten Quelle kommen, aber dann muß ich trinken, du magst sagen, was du willst:
2.20
"I will wait until we come to the next spring, but then I must drink, you may say what you like:

mein Durst ist gar zu groß.«
2.21
my thirst is too great."

2.22 Und als sie zum dritten Brünnlein kamen, hörte das Schwesterlein, wie es im Rauschen sprach:

And when they came to the third fountain, the little sister heard it murmur:

2.23 »Wer aus mir trinkt, wird ein Reh, wer aus mir trinkt, wird ein Reh.«

"Whoever drinks from me will become a deer, whoever drinks from me will become a deer."

2.24 Das Schwesterchen sprach:

The little sister said,

2.25 »Ach Brüderchen, ich bitte dich, trink nicht, sonst wirst du ein Reh und läufst mir fort.«

"Oh, brother, I beg you, don't drink or you'll become a deer and run away from me."

2.26 Aber das Brüderchen hatte sich gleich beim Brünnlein niedergekniet, hinabgebeugt und von dem Wasser getrunken und wie die ersten Tropfen auf seine Lippen gekommen waren, lag es da als ein Rehkälbchen.

But the little brother knelt down by the fountain, bent down and drank from the water, and as soon as the first drops had reached his lips, he lay there as a fawn calf.

3.1 Nun weinte das Schwesterchen über das arme verwünschte Brüderchen, und das Rehchen weinte auch und saß so traurig neben ihm.

Now the little sister wept over her poor, cursed little brother, and the little deer wept too and sat so sadly beside him.

3.2 Da sprach das Mädchen endlich:

Then at last the girl said,

»Sei still, liebes Rehchen, ich will dich ja
nimmermehr verlassen.«   3.3
"Be quiet, dear little deer, I will never leave you."

Dann band es sein goldenes Strumpfband ab und that   3.4
es dem Rehchen um den Hals,
Then she untied her golden garter and put it around the
little deer's neck,

und rupfte Binsen und flocht ein weiches Seil daraus.   3.5
and plucked rushes and wove a soft rope out of them.

Daran band es das Tierchen und führte es weiter,   3.6
He tied the little animal to it and led it on,

und ging immer tiefer in den Wald hinein.   3.7
and went deeper and deeper into the forest.

Und als sie lange, lange gegangen waren, kamen   3.8
sie endlich an ein kleines Haus, und das Mädchen
schaute hinein, und weil es leer war, dachte es,
And when they had walked for a long, long time, they
finally came to a little house, and the girl looked inside, and
because it was empty, she thought,

»Hier können wir bleiben und wohnen.«   3.9
"We can stay here and live."

3.10 Da suchte es dem Rehchen Laub und Moos zu einem weichen Lager, und jeden Morgen ging es aus und sammelte sich Wurzeln, Beeren und Nüsse, und für das Rehchen brachte es zartes Gras mit, das fraß es ihm aus der Hand, war vergnügt und spielte vor ihm herum.

So she looked for leaves and moss to make a soft bed for the little deer, and every morning she went out and gathered roots, berries and nuts, and she brought tender grass for the little deer, which she ate out of her hand, and she was happy and played around in front of him.

3.11 Abends, wenn Schwesterchen müde war und sein Gebet gesagt hatte, legte es seinen Kopf auf den Rücken des Rehkälbchens, das war sein Kissen, darauf es sanft einschlief.

In the evening, when Sis was tired and had said her prayers, she would lay her head on the back of the baby deer, which was her pillow, and gently fall asleep on it.

3.12 Und hätte das Brüderchen nur seine menschliche Gestalt gehabt,

And if only the little brother had had his human form,

3.13 es wäre ein herrliches Leben gewesen.

it would have been a wonderful life.

4.1 Das dauerte eine Zeitlang, daß sie so allein in der Wildnis waren.

It lasted for some time that they were so alone in the wilderness.

4.2 Es trug sich aber zu, daß der König des Landes eine große Jagd in dem Walde hielt.

But it happened that the king of the country was holding a great hunt in the forest.

Da schallte das Hörnerblasen, Hundegebell und das lustige Geschrei der Jäger durch die Bäume, und das Rehlein hörte es und wäre gar zu gern dabei gewesen.

The blowing of horns, the barking of dogs, and the merry shouting of the hunters resounded through the trees, and the little deer heard it, and would have loved to be there.

4.3

»Ach.« sprach es zum Schwesterlein,

"Oh." she said to her little sister,

4.4

»laß mich hinaus in die Jagd,

"let me go out hunting,

4.5

ich kann's nicht länger mehr aushalten.«

I can't stand it any longer."

4.6

und bat so lange, bis es einwilligte. »Aber.«

and she begged until she consented. "But."

4.7

sprach es zu ihm, »komm mir ja abends wieder,

said she to him, "come back to me in the evening,

4.8

vor den wilden Jägern schließ ich mein Thürlein;

I will shut my little door before the wild hunters;

4.9

und damit ich dich kenne, so klopf und sprich,

and that I may know you, knock and say,

4.10

›Mein Schwesterlein, laß mich herein,‹

'My little sister, let me in,'

4.11

und wenn du nicht so sprichst,

and if you do not say so,

4.12

so schließ ich mein Thürlein nicht auf.«

I will not open my little door."

4.13

8

4.14 Nun sprang das Rehchen hinaus und war ihm so wohl und war so lustig in freier Luft.

Now the little deer jumped out, and was so happy and merry in the open air.

4.15 Der König und seine Jäger sahen das schöne Tier und setzten ihm nach, aber sie konnten es nicht einholen, und wenn sie meinten, sie hätten es gewiß, da sprang es über das Gebüsch weg und war verschwunden.

The king and his huntsmen saw the beautiful animal and pursued it, but they could not catch it, and when they thought they had it for certain, it jumped away over the bushes and was gone.

4.16 Als es dunkel ward, lief es zu dem Häuschen, klopfte und sprach,

When it grew dark, he ran to the little house, knocked, and said,

4.17 »Mein Schwesterlein, laß mich herein.«

"My little sister, let me in."

4.18 Da ward ihm die kleine Thür aufgethan,

Then the little door was opened for her,

4.19 es sprang hinein und ruhte sich die ganze Nacht auf seinem weichen Lager aus.

she jumped in and rested all night on her soft bed.

4.20 Am anderen Morgen ging die Jagd von neuem an, und als das Rehlein wieder das Hifthorn hörte und das ho, ho!

The next morning the hunt began anew, and when the little deer heard the bugle again, and the ho, ho!

4.21 der Jäger, da hatte es keine Ruhe, und sprach,

of the hunter, she had no rest, and said,

»Schwesterchen, mach mir auf, ich muß hinaus.« 4.22
"Little sister, open the door for me, I must go out."

Das Schwesterchen öffnete ihm die Thür und sprach: 4.23
The little sister opened the door for him, and said,

»Aber zu Abend mußt du wieder da sein und dein 4.24
Sprüchlein sagen.«
"But you must be back in the evening and say your little
song."

Als der König und seine Jäger das Rehlein mit dem 4.25
goldenen Halsband wieder sahen, jagten sie ihm alle
nach, aber es war ihnen zu schnell und behend.
When the King and his huntsmen saw the little deer with
the golden collar again, they all chased after it, but it was
too quick and agile for them.

Das währte den ganzen Tag, endlich aber hatten es 4.26
die Jäger abends umzingelt, und einer verwundete
es ein wenig am Fuß, sodaß es hinken mußte und
langsam fortlief.
This lasted all day, but at last in the evening the huntsmen
had surrounded it, and one of them wounded it a little in
the foot, so that it had to limp and run slowly away.

Da schlich ihm ein Jäger nach bis zu dem Häuschen 4.27
und hörte, wie es rief,
Then a huntsman crept after her as far as the little house,
and heard her cry,

»Mein Schwesterlein, laß mich herein.« 4.28
"My little sister, let me in."

und sah, 4.29
and saw that the door was opened to him,

10

4.30 daß die Thür ihm aufgethan und alsbald wieder zugeschlossen ward.

and immediately shut again.

4.31 Der Jäger behielt das alles wohl im Sinn, ging zum König und erzählte ihm was er gesehen und gehört hatte.

The huntsman kept all this well in mind, went to the King, and told him what he had seen and heard.

4.32 Da sprach der König: »Morgen soll noch einmal gejagt werden.«

Then the king said, "Tomorrow there shall be another hunt."

5.1 Das Schwesterchen aber erschrak gewaltig, als es sah, daß sein Rehkälbchen verwundet war.

But the little sister was terrified when she saw that her baby deer was wounded.

5.2 Es wusch ihm das Blut ab, legte Kräuter auf und sprach:

She washed the blood off him, applied herbs and said,

5.3 »Geh auf dein Lager, lieb Rehchen, daß du wieder heil wirst.«

"Go to your bed, dear little deer, that you may be healed again."

5.4 Die Wunde aber war so gering, daß das Rehchen am Morgen nichts mehr davon spürte.

But the wound was so slight that the little deer felt nothing more of it in the morning.

Und als es die Jagdlust wieder draußen hörte, sprach es, 5.5

And when she again heard the hunting party outside, she said,

»Ich kann's nicht aushalten, ich muß dabei sein; 5.6

"I cannot endure it, I must be there;

sobald soll mich keiner kriegen.« 5.7

as soon as no one shall catch me."

Das Schwesterchen weinte und sprach: 5.8

The little sister wept, and said,

»Nun werden sie dich töten, und ich bin hier allein im Wald und bin verlassen von aller Welt; 5.9

"Now they will kill you, and I am here alone in the forest, and deserted by all the world;

ich laß dich nicht hinaus.« 5.10

I will not let you go out."

»So sterb ich dir hier vor Betrübnis.« antwortete das Rehchen, 5.11

"So I will die here of sorrow." answered the little deer,

»wenn ich das Hifthorn höre, so mein ich, ich müßt aus den Schuhen springen!« 5.12

"when I hear the bugle, I think I must jump out of my shoes!"

Da konnte das Schwesterchen nicht anders und schloß ihm mit schwerem Herzen die Thür auf, und das Rehchen sprang gesund und fröhlich in den Wald. 5.13

Then the little sister could not help it, and opened the door for him with a heavy heart, and the little deer sprang into the forest, healthy and happy.

5.14 Als es der König erblickte, sprach er zu seinen Jägern,
When the King saw him, he said to his huntsmen,

5.15 »Nun jagt ihm nach den ganzen Tag bis in die Nacht,
"Now chase after him all day and into the night,

5.16 aber daß ihm keiner etwas zuleide thut.«
but let no one harm him."

5.17 Sobald die Sonne untergegangen war, sprach der König zum Jäger,
As soon as the sun had set, the king said to the huntsman,

5.18 »Nun komm und zeige mir das Waldhäuschen.«
"Now come and show me the little house in the forest."

5.19 Und als er vor dem Thürlein war, klopfte er an und rief,
And when he was at the little door, he knocked and cried,

5.20 »Lieb Schwesterlein, laß mich herein.«
"Dear sister, let me in."

5.21 Da ging die Thür auf und der König trat herein, und da stand ein Mädchen, das war so schön wie er noch keins gesehen hatte.
Then the door opened and the King entered, and there stood a girl more beautiful than he had ever seen.

5.22 Das Mädchen erschrak, als es sah, daß nicht sein Rehlein, sondern ein Mann hereinkam, der eine goldene Krone auf dem Haupte hatte.
The girl was frightened when she saw that it was not her little fawn that came in, but a man with a golden crown on his head.

13

Aber der König sah es freundlich an, reichte ihm die Hand und sprach: **5.23**
But the king looked at her kindly, gave her his hand, and said,

»Willst du mit mir gehen auf mein Schloß und meine liebe Frau sein?« **5.24**
"Will you go with me to my castle and be my dear wife?"

»Ach ja.« antwortete das Mädchen, **5.25**
"Oh yes." answered the girl,

»aber das Rehchen muß auch mit, das verlaß ich nicht.« **5.26**
"but the little deer must go with me too, I won't leave her."

Sprach der König: **5.27**
Said the King,

»Es soll bei dir bleiben, solange du lebst, und soll ihm an nichts fehlen.« **5.28**
"She shall stay with you as long as you live, and shall want for nothing."

Indem kam es hereingesprungen, da band es das Schwesterchen wieder an das Binsenseil, nahm es selbst in die Hand und ging mit ihm aus dem Waldhäuschen fort. **5.29**
Then she jumped in, tied the little sister to the rush rope again, took her in her own hand, and went away with her from the little house in the forest.

6.1 Der König nahm das schöne Mädchen auf sein Pferd und führte es in sein Schloß, wo die Hochzeit mit großer Pracht gefeiert wurde, und war es nun die Frau Königin, und lebten sie lange Zeit vergnügt zusammen;

The king took the beautiful girl on his horse and led her to his castle, where the wedding was celebrated with great splendor, and now she was the queen, and they lived happily together for a long time;

6.2 das Rehlein ward gehegt und gepflegt und sprang in dem Schloßgarten herum.

the little deer was nursed and cared for and jumped about in the castle garden.

6.3 Die böse Stiefmutter aber, um derentwillen die Kinder in die Welt hineingegangen waren, die meinte nicht anders, als Schwesterchen wäre von den wilden Tieren im Walde zerrissen worden und Brüderchen als ein Rehkalb von den Jägern totgeschossen.

But the wicked stepmother, for whose sake the children had gone into the world, did not think otherwise than that little sister had been torn to pieces by the wild beasts in the forest, and little brother shot dead by the hunters as a fawn.

6.4 Als sie nun hörte, daß sie so glücklich waren und es ihnen so wohl ging, da wurden Neid und Mißgunst in ihrem Herzen rege und ließen ihr keine Ruhe, und sie hatte keinen anderen Gedanken, als wie sie die beiden doch noch ins Unglück bringen könnte.

When she heard that they were so happy and so well off, envy and resentment stirred in her heart and left her no peace, and she had no other thought than how she could bring them both to misfortune.

Ihre rechte Tochter, die häßlich war wie die Nacht, und nur ein Auge hatte, die machte ihr Vorwürfe und sprach: 6.5
Her right-hand daughter, who was as ugly as night, and had only one eye, reproached her, and said,

»Eine Königin zu werden, das Glück hätte mir gebührt.«   6.6
"To become a queen would have been my good fortune."

»Sei nur still.« sagte die Alte und sprach sie zufrieden,   6.7
"Be quiet." said the old woman, and she spoke contentedly,

»wenn's Zeit ist, will ich schon bei der Hand sein.«   6.8
"when the time comes, I will be at hand."

Als nun die Zeit herangerückt war, und die Königin ein schönes Knäblein zur Welt gebracht hatte, und der König gerade auf der Jagd war, nahm die alte Hexe die Gestalt der Kammerfrau an, trat in die Stube, wo die Königin lag und sprach zu der Kranken: 6.9
When the time had come, and the queen had given birth to a beautiful baby, and the king was out hunting, the old witch took the form of the chambermaid, entered the room where the queen was lying, and said to the sick woman,

»Kommt, das Bad ist fertig, das wird Euch wohlthun und frische Kräfte geben: 6.10
"Come, the bath is ready, it will do you good and give you fresh strength:

geschwind, ehe es kalt wird.«   6.11
quickly, before it gets cold."

Ihre Tochter war auch bei der Hand,   6.12
Her daughter was also at hand,

6.13 sie trugen nun die schwache Königin in die Badestube und legten sie in die Wanne: dann schlossen sie die Thür ab und liefen davon.

and they carried the weak queen into the bathing-room and laid her in the tub; then they locked the door and ran away.

6.14 In der Badestube aber hatten sie ein rechtes Höllenfeuer angemacht,

But in the bathing-room they had kindled a hell-fire,

6.15 daß die schöne junge Königin bald ersticken mußte.

so that the beautiful young queen was soon suffocated.

7.1 Als das vollbracht war, nahm die Alte ihre Tochter, setzte ihr eine Haube auf und legte sie ins Bett an der Königin Stelle.

When this was done, the old woman took her daughter, put a hood on her head and laid her in bed in the queen's place.

7.2 Sie gab ihr auch die Gestalt und das Ansehen der Königin,

She also gave her the form and appearance of the queen,

7.3 nur das verlorene Auge konnte sie ihr nicht wiedergeben.

but she could not give her back her lost eye.

7.4 Damit es aber der König nicht merkte, mußte sie sich auf die Seite legen, wo sie kein Auge hatte.

But to prevent the king from noticing it, she had to lie down on her side where she had no eye.

Am Abend, als er heimkam und hörte, daß ihm ein   7.5
Söhnlein geboren war, freute er sich herzlich, und
wollte ans Bett seiner lieben Frau gehen und sehen
was sie machte.

In the evening, when he came home and heard that a little
son had been born to him, he rejoiced heartily, and wanted
to go to his dear wife's bedside and see what she was doing.

Da rief die Alte geschwind: 7.6

Then the old woman called quickly,

»Beileibe, laßt die Vorhänge zu, die Königin darf   7.7
noch nicht ins Licht sehen und muß Ruhe haben.«

"By all means, let the curtains be drawn, the queen must
not yet see the light, and must have rest."

Der König ging zurück und wußte nicht, daß eine   7.8
falsche Königin im Bette lag.

The king went back and did not know that a false queen was
lying in bed.

Als es aber Mitternacht war und alles schlief, da   8.1
sah die Kinderfrau, die in der Kinderstube neben
der Wiege saß und allein noch wachte, wie die Thür
aufging, und die rechte Königin hereintrat.

But when it was midnight and everyone was asleep, the
nanny, who was sitting in the nursery next to the cradle
and was still awake alone, saw the door open and the right-
hand queen enter.

Sie nahm das Kind aus der Wiege,   8.2

She took the child out of the cradle,

legte es in ihren Arm und gab ihm zu trinken.   8.3

put it in her arms and gave it a drink.

8.4 Dann schüttelte sie ihm sein Kißchen, legte es wieder hinein und deckte es mit dem Deckbettchen zu.

Then she shook his little pillow, put him in again, and covered him with the blanket

8.5 Sie vergaß aber auch das Rehchen nicht, ging in die Ecke, wo es lag und streichelte ihm über den Rücken.

But she did not forget the little deer, went to the corner where it lay and stroked its back.

8.6 Darauf ging sie ganz stillschweigend wieder zur Thür hinaus und die Kinderfrau fragte am anderen Morgen die Wächter, ob jemand während der Nacht ins Schloß gegangen wäre, aber sie antworteten,

Then she went quietly out of the door again, and the next morning the nanny asked the watchmen if anyone had gone into the castle during the night, but they replied,

8.7 »Nein, wir haben niemand gesehen.«

"No, we have seen no one."

8.8 So kam sie viele Nächte und sprach niemals ein Wort dabei:

So she came many nights and never said a word:

8.9 die Kinderfrau sah sie immer, aber sie getraute sich nicht, jemand etwas davon zu sagen.

the nanny always saw her, but she dared not tell anyone.

9.1 Als nun so eine Zeit verflossen war,

When some time had passed,

9.2 da hub die Königin in der Nacht an zu reden und sprach:

the queen began to speak in the night and said:

»Was macht mein Kind?
was macht mein Reh?

"What is my child doing?
What is my deer doing?

Nun komm ich noch
zweimal und dann
nimmermehr.«

Now I'll come twice
more and then never
again."

Die Kinderfrau antwortete ihr nicht, aber als sie
wieder verschwunden war, ging sie zum König und
erzählte ihm alles.

11.1

The nanny did not answer her, but when she had
disappeared again, she went to the king and told him
everything.

Sprach der König: »Ach Gott, was ist das!

11.2

The king said, "Oh, God, what is this!

ich will in der nächsten Nacht bei dem Kinde
wachen.«

11.3

I will keep watch over the child the next night."

Abends ging er in die Kinderstube,

11.4

In the evening he went into the nursery,

aber um Mitternacht erschien die Königin wieder
und sprach:

11.5

but at midnight the queen appeared again and said:

»Was macht mein Kind?
was macht mein Reh?

"What is my child doing?
What is my deer doing?

Nun komm ich noch einmal
und dann nimmermehr.«

Now I'll come once more
and then never again."

13.1 Und pflegte dann des Kindes, wie sie gewöhnlich that, ehe sie verschwand.

And then she nursed the child, as she usually did, before she disappeared.

13.2 Der König getraute sich nicht sie anzureden,

The king dared not speak to her,

13.3 aber er wachte auch in der folgenden Nacht.

but he kept watch the next night.

13.4 Sie sprach abermals:

She spoke again:

»Was macht mein Kind? was macht mein Reh?	"What is my child doing? What is my deer doing?
Nun komm ich noch diesmal und dann nimmermehr.«	Now I'll come this time and then never again."

15.1 Da konnte sich der König nicht zurückhalten, sprang zu ihr und sprach,

Then the king could not restrain himself, jumped up to her and said,

15.2 »Du kannst niemand anders sein als meine liebe Frau.«

"You can be no other than my dear wife."

15.3 Da antwortete sie: »Ja, ich bin deine liebe Frau.«

She answered, "Yes, I am your dear wife."

15.4 und hatte in dem Augenblick durch Gottes Gnade das Leben wieder erhalten, war frisch, rot und gesund.

and at that moment, by the grace of God, she had regained her life and was fresh, red and healthy.

Darauf erzählte sie dem König den Frevel, den die
böse Hexe und ihre Tochter an ihr verübt hatten. 15.5
She then told the king of the outrage that the wicked witch
and her daughter had committed against her.

Der König ließ beide vor Gericht führen, und es ward
ihnen das Urteil gesprochen. 15.6
The king had them both brought to court and they were
sentenced.

Die Tochter ward in den Wald geführt, wo sie die
wilden Tiere zerrissen, die Hexe aber ward ins Feuer
gelegt und mußte jammervoll verbrennen. 15.7
The daughter was led into the forest, where the wild
animals tore her to pieces, but the witch was put into the
fire and had to burn miserably.

Und wie sie zu Asche verbrannt war, 15.8
And when she was burnt to ashes,

verwandelte sich das Rehkälbchen und erhielt seine
menschliche Gestalt wieder: 15.9
the little deer calf was transformed and regained its human
form:

Schwesterchen und Brüderchen aber lebten glücklich
zusammen bis an ihr Ende. 15.10
but sister and brother lived happily together to the end.

Der Bärenhäuter

The Bear Skinner

1.1 Es war einmal ein junger Kerl, der ließ sich als Soldat anwerben, hielt sich tapfer und war immer der vorderste, wenn es blaue Bohnen regnete.

Once upon a time there was a young lad who enlisted as a soldier, stood his ground bravely and was always at the front when it rained blue beans.

1.2 Solange der Krieg dauerte, ging alles gut, aber als Friede geschlossen war, erhielt er seinen Abschied, und der Hauptmann sagte, er könnte gehen wohin er wollte.

As long as the war lasted, everything went well, but when peace was made, he was given his leave and the captain said he could go wherever he wanted.

1.3 Seine Eltern waren tot, und er hatte keine Heimat mehr, da ging er zu seinen Brüdern und bat, sie möchten ihm so lange Unterhalt geben, bis der Krieg wieder anfinge.

His parents were dead and he no longer had a home, so he went to his brothers and asked them to support him until the war started again.

Die Brüder aber waren hartherzig und sagten: 1.4
But the brothers were hard-hearted and said:

»Was sollen wir mit dir? 1.5
"What should we do with you?

Wir können dich nicht brauchen, sieh zu, wie du dich 1.6
durchschlägst.«
We can't use you, see how you get by."

Der Soldat hatte nichts übrig als sein Gewehr, 1.7
The soldier had nothing left but his rifle,

das nahm er auf die Schulter und wollte in die Welt 1.8
gehen.
which he took on his shoulder and wanted to go out into
the world.

Er kam auf eine große Heide, auf der nichts zu sehen 1.9
war als ein Ring von Bäumen:
He came to a large heath where there was nothing to be
seen but a ring of trees:

darunter setzte er sich ganz traurig nieder und sann 1.10
über sein Schicksal nach.
he sat down sadly beneath it and pondered his fate.

»Ich habe kein Geld.« dachte er, 1.11
"I have no money." he thought,

»ich habe nichts gelernt als das Kriegshandwerk, 1.12
"I have learned nothing but the trade of war,

und jetzt weil Friede geschlossen ist brauchen sie 1.13
mich nicht mehr;
and now that peace has been made they no longer need me;

1.14 ich sehe voraus, ich muß verhungern.«

I foresee that I must starve."

1.15 Auf einmal hörte er ein Brausen und wie er sich umblickte, stand ein unbekannter Mann vor ihm, der einen grünen Rock trug, recht stattlich aussah, aber einen garstigen Pferdefuß hatte.

Suddenly he heard a roar, and as he looked around, an unknown man stood before him, wearing a green coat, looking quite handsome, but with a nasty horse's foot.

1.16 »Ich weiß schon was dir fehlt.« sagte der Mann,

"I already know what you lack." said the man,

1.17 »Geld und Gut sollst du haben, so viel du mit aller Gewalt durchbringen kannst, aber ich muß zuvor wissen ob du dich nicht fürchtest, damit ich mein Geld nicht umsonst ausgebe.«

"money and goods you shall have, as much as you can get away with, but I must first know whether you are not afraid, so that I do not spend my money in vain."

1.18 »Ein Soldat und Furcht, wie paßt das zusammen?« antwortete er,

"A soldier and fear, how do they go together?" he replied,

1.19 »du kannst mich auf die Probe stellen.«

"you can put me to the test."

1.20 »Wohlan.« antwortete der Mann, »schau hinter dich.«

"Very well." replied the man, "look behind you."

1.21 Der Soldat kehrte sich um und sah einen großen Bär, der brummend auf ihn zutrabte.

The soldier turned around and saw a large bear growling as it crawled towards him.

»Oho.« rief der Soldat,
1.22
"Oho." shouted the soldier,

»dich will ich an der Nase kitzeln, daß dir die Lust
zum Brummen vergehen soll.«
1.23
"I will tickle your nose so that you lose your desire to
growl."

legte an und schoß den Bär auf die Schnauze, daß er
zusammenfiel und sich nicht mehr regte.
1.24
The soldier started up and shot the bear on the snout so that
he fell down and stopped moving.

»Ich sehe wohl.« sagte der Fremde,
1.25
"I see." said the stranger,

»daß dir's an Mut nicht fehlt, aber es ist noch eine
Bedingung dabei, die mußt du erfüllen.«
1.26
"that you are not lacking in courage, but there is one more
condition, which you must fulfill."

»Wenn mir's an meiner Seligkeit nicht schadet.«
1.27
"If it does me no harm in my happiness."

antwortete der Soldat, der wohl merkte, wen er vor
sich hatte,
1.28
replied the soldier, who well realized whom he had before
him,

»sonst laß ich mich auf nichts ein.«
1.29
"otherwise I will not agree to anything."

»Das wirst du selber sehen.« antwortete der
Grünrock,
1.30
"You will see for yourself." replied the greencoat,

1.31 »du darfst in den nächsten sieben Jahren dich nicht waschen, dir Bart und Haare nicht kämmen, die Nägel nicht schneiden und kein Vaterunser beten.

"for the next seven years you must not wash yourself, comb your beard and hair, cut your nails or pray the Lord's Prayer.

1.32 Dann will ich dir einen Rock und Mantel geben,

Then I will give you a coat and cloak,

1.33 den mußt du in dieser Zeit tragen.

which you must wear during this time.

1.34 Stirbst du in diesen sieben Jahren, so bist du mein, bleibst du aber leben, so bist du frei und bist reich dazu für dein Lebtag.«

If you die during these seven years, you are mine, but if you live, you are free and rich for life."

1.35 Der Soldat dachte an die große Not, in der er sich befand, und da er so oft in den Tod gegangen war, wollte er es auch jetzt wagen und willigte ein.

The soldier thought of the great need he was in, and as he had gone to his death so often, he wanted to dare to do so now and agreed.

1.36 Der Teufel zog den grünen Rock aus, reichte ihn dem Soldaten hin und sagte:

The devil took off the green coat, handed it to the soldier and said,

1.37 »Wenn du den Rock an deinem Leibe hast und in die Tasche greifst,

"If you keep the coat on your body and reach into your pocket,

so wirst du die Hand immer voll Geld haben.«   1.38

you will always have your hand full of money."

Dann zog er dem Bären die Haut ab und sagte,   1.39

Then he pulled off the bear's skin and said,

»Das soll dein Mantel sein und auch dein Bett,   1.40

"This shall be your coat and also your bed,

denn darauf mußt du schlafen und darfst in kein   1.41
anderes Bett kommen.

for you must sleep on it and not get into any other bed.

Und dieser Tracht wegen sollst du Bärenhäuter   1.42
heißen.«

And because of this garment you shall be called Bearskin."

Hierauf verschwand der Teufel.   1.43

Then the devil disappeared.

Der Soldat zog den Rock an, griff gleich in die Tasche   2.1
und fand, daß die Sache ihre Richtigkeit hatte.

The soldier put on his coat, immediately reached into his
pocket and found that the matter was right.

Dann hing er die Bärenhaut um, ging in die Welt, war   2.2
guter Dinge und unterließ nichts, was ihm wohl und
dem Gelde wehe that.

Then he put on the bearskin, went out into the world, was
in good spirits and did nothing that was good for him or
bad for the money.

Im ersten Jahr ging es noch leidlich,   2.3

In the first year things went well,

2.4 aber in dem zweiten sah er schon aus wie ein Ungeheuer.

but in the second he looked like a monster.

2.5 Das Haar bedeckte ihm fast das ganze Gesicht, sein Bart glich einem Stück grobem Filztuch, seine Finger hatten Krallen, und sein Gesicht war so mit Schmutz bedeckt, daß, wenn man Kresse hineingesät hätte, sie aufgegangen wäre.

His hair covered almost his whole face, his beard resembled a piece of coarse felt cloth, his fingers had claws, and his face was so covered with dirt that if you had sown cress in it, it would have sprouted.

2.6 Wer ihn sah, lief fort; weil er aber allerorten den Armen Geld gab, damit sie für ihn beteten, daß er in den sieben Jahren nicht stürbe, und weil er alles gut bezahlte, so erhielt er doch immer noch Herberge.

Anyone who saw him ran away, but because he gave money to the poor everywhere so that they would pray for him so that he would not die during the seven years, and because he paid well for everything, he was still given shelter.

2.7 Im vierten Jahr kam er in ein Wirtshaus, da wollte ihn der Wirt nicht aufnehmen und wollte ihm nicht einmal einen Platz im Stall anweisen, weil er fürchtete, seine Pferde würden scheu werden.

In his fourth year he came to an inn, where the landlord refused to take him in and would not even give him a place in the stable for fear that his horses would become shy.

Doch als der Bärenhäuter in die Tasche griff und eine Hand voll Dukaten herausholte, so ließ der Wirt sich erweichen, und gab ihm eine Stube im Hintergebäude; doch mußte er versprechen, sich nicht sehen zu lassen, damit sein Haus nicht in bösen Ruf käme.

2.8

But when the bearskinner reached into his pocket and took out a handful of ducats, the innkeeper relented and gave him a room in the back building, but he had to promise not to show his face so that his house would not get a bad reputation.

Als der Bärenhäuter abends allein saß und von Herzen wünschte, daß die sieben Jahre herum wären, so hörte er in einem Nebenzimmer ein lautes Jammern.

3.1

As the bearskinner sat alone in the evening, wishing with all his heart that the seven years were over, he heard a loud wailing in an adjoining room.

Er hatte ein mitleidiges Herz, öffnete die Thür und erblickte einen alten Mann, der heftig weinte und die Hände über dem Kopf zusammenschlug.

3.2

He had a compassionate heart, opened the door and saw an old man weeping violently and beating his hands over his head.

Der Bärenhäuter trat näher,

3.3

The bearskinner came closer,

aber der Mann sprang auf und wollte entfliehen.

3.4

but the man jumped up and wanted to escape.

3.5 Endlich, als er eine menschliche Stimme vernahm, ließ er sich bewegen, und durch freundliches Zureden brachte es der Bärenhäuter dahin, daß er ihm die Ursache seines Kummers offenbarte.

At last, when he heard a human voice, he allowed himself to be moved, and by friendly persuasion the bearskinner made him reveal the cause of his grief.

3.6 Sein Vermögen war nach und nach geschwunden, er und seine Töchter mußten darben, und er war so arm, daß er den Wirt nicht einmal bezahlen konnte und ins Gefängnis sollte gesetzt werden.

His fortune had gradually dwindled, he and his daughters were destitute, and he was so poor that he could not even pay the innkeeper and was to be put in prison.

3.7 »Wenn Ihr weiter keine Sorgen habt.« sagte der Bärenhäuter,

"If you have no more worries." said the bearskinner,

3.8 »Geld habe ich genug.« Er ließ den Wirt herbeikommen,

"I have enough money." He sent for the innkeeper,

3.9 bezahlte ihn und steckte dem Unglücklichen noch einen Beutel voll Gold in die Tasche.

paid him and put another bag of gold in the unfortunate man's pocket.

4.1 Als der alte Mann sich aus seinen Sorgen erlöst sah, wußte er nicht, womit er sich dankbar beweisen sollte.

When the old man saw himself relieved of his worries, he did not know what he should do to show his gratitude.

4.2 »Komm mit mir.« sprach er zu ihm,

"Come with me." he said to him,

31

»meine Töchter sind Wunder von Schönheit, 4.3
"my daughters are wonders of beauty,

wähle dir eine davon zur Frau. 4.4
choose one of them as your wife.

Wenn sie hört, was du für mich gethan hast, so wird 4.5
sie sich nicht weigern.
When she hears what you have done for me, she will not
refuse.

Du siehst freilich ein wenig seltsam aus, 4.6
You may look a little strange,

aber sie wird dich schon wieder in Ordnung 4.7
bringen.«
but she will put you right."

Dem Bärenhäuter gefiel das wohl und er ging mit. 4.8
The bearskin liked that and went along.

Als ihn die älteste erblickte, entsetzte sie sich so 4.9
gewaltig vor seinem Antlitz, daß sie aufschrie und
fort lief.
When the eldest saw him, she was so horrified by his face
that she cried out and ran away.

Die zweite blieb zwar stehen und betrachtete ihn von 4.10
Kopf bis zu Füßen, dann aber sprach sie:
The second stopped and looked at him from head to foot,
but then she said,

»Wie kann ich einen Mann nehmen, der keine 4.11
menschliche Gestalt mehr hat?
"How can I take a man who no longer has a human form?

4.12 Da gefiel mir der rasierte Bär noch besser, der einmal hier zu sehen war und sich für einen Menschen ausgab, der hatte doch einen Husarenpelz an und weiße Handschuhe.

I liked the shaved bear even better, who was once seen here and pretended to be a human being, but he was wearing a hussar's coat and white gloves.

4.13 Wenn er nur häßlich wäre, so könnte ich mich an ihn gewöhnen.«

If only he were ugly, I could get used to him."

4.14 Die jüngste aber sprach:

But the youngest said,

4.15 »Lieber Vater, das muß ein guter Mann sein, der Euch aus der Not geholfen hat, habt Ihr ihm dafür eine Braut versprochen, so muß Euer Wort gehalten werden.«

"Dear father, that must be a good man who has helped you out of trouble, and if you have promised him a bride in return, your word must be kept."

4.16 Es war schade, daß das Gesicht des Bärenhäuters von Schmutz und Haaren bedeckt war, sonst hätte man sehen können wie ihm das Herz im Leibe lachte, als er diese Worte hörte.

It was a pity that the bearskin's face was covered with dirt and hair, otherwise one could have seen how his heart laughed in his body when he heard these words.

4.17 Er nahm einen Ring von seinem Finger, brach ihn entzwei und gab ihr die eine Hälfte, die andere behielt er für sich.

He took a ring from his finger, broke it in two and gave her one half, keeping the other for himself.

In ihre Hälfte aber schrieb er seinen Namen und in
seine Hälfte schrieb er ihren Namen und bat sie ihr
Stück gut aufzuheben.

4.18

But in her half he wrote his name and in his half he wrote
her name and asked her to take good care of her piece.

Hierauf nahm er Abschied und sprach:

4.19

Then he took his leave and said,

»Ich muss noch drei Jahre wandern, komm ich aber
nicht wieder, so bist du frei, weil ich dann tot bin.

4.20

"I must wander for another three years, but if I do not come
back, you will be free, because I will be dead.

Bitte aber Gott, daß er mir das Leben erhält.«

4.21

But ask God to preserve my life."

Die arme Braut kleidete sich ganz schwarz, und wenn
sie an ihren Bräutigam dachte, so kamen ihr die
Thränen in die Augen.

5.1

The poor bride dressed all in black, and when she thought
of her bridegroom, tears came to her eyes.

Von ihren Schwestern ward ihr nichts als Hohn und
Spott zu teil.

5.2

She received nothing but scorn and ridicule from her
sisters.

»Nimm dich in acht.« sprach die älteste,

5.3

"Take care." said the eldest,

»wenn du ihm die Hand reichst,

5.4

"if you shake hands with him,

so schlägt er dir mit der Tatze darauf.«

5.5

he will strike you with his paw."

5.6 »Hüte dich.« sagte die zweite,

"Beware." said the second,

5.7 »die Bären lieben die Süßigkeit, und wenn du ihm gefällst, so frißt er dich auf.«

"the bears love sweetness, and if you please him, he will eat you up."

5.8 »Du mußt nur immer seinen Willen thun.«

"You must always do his bidding."

5.9 hob die älteste wieder an, »sonst fängt er an zu brummen.«

resumed the eldest, "or he will begin to growl."

5.10 Und die zweite fuhr fort:

And the second continued:

5.11 »Aber die Hochzeit wird lustig sein, Bären die tanzen gut.«

"But the wedding will be fun, bears dance well."

5.12 Die Braut schwieg still und ließ sich nicht irre machen.

The bride remained silent and did not allow herself to be misled.

5.13 Der Bärenhäuter aber zog in der Welt herum, von einem Ort zum anderen, that Gutes, wo er konnte und gab den Armen reichlich, damit sie für ihn beteten.

But the bearskinner went about the world, from one place to another, doing good wherever he could and giving generously to the poor so that they would pray for him.

Endlich als der letzte Tag von den sieben Jahren
anbrach, ging er wieder hinaus auf die Heide und
setzte sich unter den Ring von Bäumen.
5.14

Finally, when the last day of the seven years dawned, he
went out onto the heath again and sat down under the ring
of trees.

Nicht lange, so sauste der Wind, und der Teufel stand
vor ihm und blickte ihn verdrießlich an;
5.15

It was not long before the wind blew and the devil stood
before him and looked at him glumly;

dann warf er ihm den alten Rock hin und verlangte
seinen grünen zurück.
5.16

then he threw him his old coat and demanded his green one
back.

»So weit sind wir noch nicht.« antwortete der
Bärenhäuter,
5.17

"We're not that far yet." replied the bearskinner,

»erst sollst du mich reinigen.«
5.18

"first you have to cleanse me."

Der Teufel mochte wollen oder nicht, er mußte
Wasser holen, den Bärenhäuter abwaschen, ihm
die Haare kämmen und die Nägel schneiden.
5.19

Whether the devil wanted to or not, he had to fetch water,
wash the bearskin, comb his hair and cut his nails.

Hierauf sah er wie ein tapferer Kriegsmann aus und
war viel schöner als je vorher.
5.20

Then he looked like a brave man of war and was much more
beautiful than ever before.

Als der Teufel glücklich abgezogen war,
6.1

When the devil had happily departed,

6.2 so war es dem Bärenhäuter ganz leicht ums Herz.

the bearskinner's heart was very light.

6.3 Er ging in die Stadt, that einen prächtigen Sammetrock an, setzte sich in einen Wagen mit vier Schimmeln bespannt und fuhr zu dem Hause seiner Braut.

He went into the town, put on a splendid velvet coat, got into a carriage drawn by four white horses and drove to his bride's house.

6.4 Niemand erkannte ihn, der Vater hielt ihn für einen vornehmen Feldoberst und führte ihn in das Zimmer, wo seine Töchter saßen.

No one recognized him; his father took him for a distinguished colonel and led him into the room where his daughters were sitting.

6.5 Er mußte sich zwischen den beiden ältesten niederlassen:

He was made to sit down between the two eldest:

6.6 sie schenkten ihm Wein ein, legten ihm die besten Bissen vor und meinten, sie hätten keinen schöneren Mann auf der Welt gesehen.

they poured him wine, set the best morsels before him, and said they had never seen a handsomer man in the world.

6.7 Die Braut aber saß in schwarzem Kleide ihm gegenüber, schlug die Augen nicht auf und sprach kein Wort.

The bride, however, sat opposite him in a black dress, did not open her eyes or speak a word.

Als er endlich den Vater fragte, ob er ihm eine 6.8
seiner Töchter zur Frau geben wollte, so sprangen
die beiden ältesten auf, liefen in ihre Kammer und
wollten prächtige Kleider anziehen, denn eine jede
bildete sich ein, sie wäre die Auserwählte.

When he finally asked the father if he would give him one
of his daughters in marriage, the two eldest jumped up, ran
into their chamber and wanted to put on splendid clothes,
for each of them imagined that she was the chosen one.

Der Fremde, sobald er mit seiner Braut allein war, 6.9
holte den halben Ring hervor und warf ihn in einem
Becher mit Wein, den er ihr über den Tisch reichte.

The stranger, as soon as he was alone with his bride, took
out half the ring and threw it into a cup of wine, which he
handed to her across the table.

Sie nahm ihn an, aber als sie getrunken hatte und den 6.10
halbem Ring auf dem Grund liegen fand, so schlug
ihr das Herz.

She accepted it, but when she had drunk and found the half
ring lying at the bottom, her heart sank.

Sie holte die andere Hälfte, die sie an einem Band um 6.11
den Hals trug, hielt sie daran, und es zeigte sich, daß
beide Teile vollkommen zu einander paßten.

She fetched the other half, which she wore on a ribbon
round her neck, held it to it, and it turned out that the two
parts fitted each other perfectly.

Da sprach er: 6.12

Then he said,

6.13 »Ich bin dein verlobter Bräutigam, den du als Bärenhäuter gesehen hast, aber durch Gottes Gnade habe ich meine menschliche Gestalt wieder erhalten und bin wieder rein geworden.«

"I am your betrothed bridegroom, whom you saw as a bearskin, but by the grace of God I have regained my human form and have become pure again."

6.14 Er ging auf sie zu, umarmte sie und gab ihr einen Kuß.

He went up to her, embraced her and gave her a kiss.

6.15 Indem kamen die beiden Schwestern in vollem Putz herein, und als sie sahen, daß der schöne Mann der jüngsten zu teil geworden war und hörten, daß das der Bärenhäuter war, liefen sie voll Zorn und Wut hinaus;

Then the two sisters came in in full finery, and when they saw that the handsome man had been given to the youngest, and heard that it was the bear-skinner, they ran out full of anger and rage;

6.16 die eine ersäufte sich im Brunnen,

one drowned herself in the well,

6.17 die andere erhängte sich an einem Baum.

the other hanged herself from a tree.

6.18 Am Abend klopfte jemand an der Thür, und als der Bräutigam öffnete, so war's der Teufel im grünen Rock, der sprach,

In the evening someone knocked at the door, and when the bridegroom opened it, it was the devil in the green robe, who said,

6.19 »Siehst du, nun habe ich zwei Seelen für deine eine.«

"See, now I have two souls for your one."

39

Der Zaunkönig und der Bär

The Wren and the Bear

1.1 Zur Sommerszeit gingen einmal der Bär und der Wolf im Walde spazieren, da hörte der Bär so schönen Gesang von einem Vogel und sprach:
Once, in the summertime, the bear and the wolf were walking in the forest when the bear heard a bird singing so beautifully and said:

1.2 »Bruder Wolf, was ist das für ein Vogel, der so schön singt?«
"Brother wolf, what is that bird that sings so beautifully?"

1.3 »Das ist der König der Vögel.« sagte der Wolf,
"That's the king of birds." said the wolf,

1.4 »vor dem müssen wir uns neigen.« es war aber der Zaunkönig.
"we must bow down to him." But it was the wren.

1.5 »Wenn das ist.« sagte der Bär,
"If it is." said the bear,

1.6 »so möcht ich auch gern seinen königlichen Palast sehen,
"I should like to see his royal palace,

komm und führe mich hin.« 1.7
come and take me there."

»Das geht nicht so, wie du meinst.« sprach der Wolf, 1.8
"That won't do as you think." said the wolf,

»du mußt warten, bis die Frau Königin kommt.« 1.9
"you must wait until the queen comes."

Bald darauf kam die Frau Königin und hatte Futter 1.10
im Schnabel, und der Herr König auch, und wollten
ihre Jungen ätzen.
Soon after, the queen came and had food in her beak, and
the king too, and wanted to eat her cubs.

Der Bär wäre gern nun gleich hinterdrein gegangen, 1.11
aber der Wolf hielt ihn am Ärmel und sagte:
The bear would have liked to go in right away, but the wolf
held him by the sleeve and said,

»Nein, du mußt warten, bis Herr und Frau Königin 1.12
wieder fort sind.«
"No, you must wait until Mr. and Mrs. Queen are gone
again."

Also nahmen sie das Loch in acht, wo das Nest stand, 1.13
und trabten wieder ab.
So they took care of the hole where the nest was and trotted
off again.

Der Bär aber hatte keine Ruhe, wollte den 1.14
königlichen Palast sehen, und ging nach einer kurzen
Weile wieder vor.
But the bear had no rest, wanted to see the royal palace, and
after a short while went forward again.

1.15 Da waren König und Königin richtig ausgeflogen:
Then the king and queen had really flown out:

1.16 er guckte hinein und sah fünf oder sechs Junge, die lagen darin.
he looked inside and saw five or six cubs lying there.

1.17 »Ist das der königliche Palast!« rief der Bär,
"Is this the royal palace!" cried the bear,

1.18 »das ist ein erbärmlicher Palast!
"this is a miserable palace!

1.19 Ihr seid auch keine Königskinder, ihr seid unehrliche Kinder.«
You are not royal children either, you are dishonest children."

1.20 Wie das die jungen Zaunkönige hörten, wurden sie gewaltig böse, und schrien,
When the young wrens heard this, they became very angry and shouted,

1.21 »Nein, das sind wir nicht, unsere Eltern sind ehrliche Leute;
"No, we are not, our parents are honest people;

1.22 Bär, das soll ausgemacht werden mit dir.«
Bear, this shall be settled with you."

1.23 Dem Bär und dem Wolf ward angst, sie kehrten um und setzten sich in ihre Höhlen.
The bear and the wolf were frightened and turned back and sat down in their dens.

Die jungen Zaunkönige aber schrien und lärmten fort, und als ihre Eltern wieder Futter brachten, sagten sie, 1.24
But the young wrens continued to shout and make a noise, and when their parents brought food again, they said,

»Wir rühren kein Fliegenbeinchen an und sollten wir verhungern, 1.25
"We will not touch a fly's leg,

bis ihr erst ausgemacht habt ob wir ehrliche Kinder sind oder nicht: 1.26
and we shall starve until you have made out whether we are honest children or not:

der Bär ist dagewesen und hat uns gescholten.« 1.27
the bear has been there and scolded us."

Da sagte der alte König: »Seid nur ruhig, 1.28
Then the old king said, "Be quiet,

das soll ausgemacht werden.« 1.29
that shall be settled."

Flog darauf mit der Frau Königin dem Bären vor seine Höhle und rief hinein: 1.30
Then he and the queen flew to the bear's cave and called inside:

»Alter Brummbär, warum hast du meine Kinder gescholten? 1.31
"Old grumpy bear, why did you scold my children?

Das soll dir übel bekommen, 1.32
This shall be bad for you,

das wollen wir in einem blutigen Kriege ausmachen.« 1.33
we will settle this in a bloody war."

44

1.34 Also war dem Bären der Krieg angekündigt, und ward alles vierfüßige Getier berufen, Ochs, Esel, Rind, Hirsch, Reh, und was die Erde sonst alles trägt.

So war was announced to the bear, and all four-footed animals were summoned, ox, ass, ox, stag, deer, and whatever else the earth bears.

1.35 Der Zaunkönig aber berief alles was in der Luft fliegt;

But the wren summoned everything that flies in the air;

1.36 nicht allein die Vögel groß und klein, sondern auch die Mücken, Hornissen, Bienen und Fliegen mußten herbei.

not only the birds large and small, but also the gnats, hornets, bees and flies had to come.

2.1 Als nun die Zeit kam, wo der Krieg angehen sollte, da schickte der Zaunkönig Kundschafter aus, wer der kommandierende General des Feindes wäre.

When the time came for the war to begin, the wren sent out scouts to find out who the enemy's commanding general was.

2.2 Die Mücke war die listigste von allen, schwärmte im Walde, wo der Feind sich versammelte, und setzte sich endlich unter ein Blatt auf den Baum, wo die Parole ausgegeben wurde.

The mosquito was the most cunning of all, swarmed into the forest where the enemy was gathering, and finally sat down under a leaf on the tree where the slogan was given out.

2.3 Da stand der Bär, rief den Fuchs vor sich und sprach:

Then the bear stood, called the fox before him, and said,

»Fuchs, du bist der schlaueste unter allem Getier, du sollst General sein und uns anführen.«   2.4

"Fox, you are the most cunning of all animals, you shall be general and lead us."

»Gut.« sagte der Fuchs,   2.5

"Very well." said the fox,

»aber was für Zeichen wollen wir verabreden?« Niemand wußte es.   2.6

"but what sign shall we make?" No one knew.

Da sprach der Fuchs,   2.7

Then the fox said,

»Ich habe einen schönen langen buschigen Schwanz,   2.8

"I have a beautiful long bushy tail,

der sieht aus fast wie ein roter Federbusch;   2.9

which looks almost like a red plume;

wenn ich den Schwanz in die Höhe halte, so geht die Sache gut, und ihr müßt darauf los marschieren;   2.10

if I hold up my tail, things will go well, and you must march on it;

laß ich ihn aber herunterhängen, so lauft was ihr könnt.«   2.11

but if I let it hang down, run as fast as you can."

Als die Mücke das gehört hatte,   2.12

When the gnat had heard this,

flog sie wieder heim und verriet dem Zaunkönig alles haarklein.   2.13

he flew home again and told the wren everything in detail.

3.1 Als der Tag anbrach, wo die Schlacht sollte
geliefert werden, hu, da kam das vierfüßige Getier
dahergerannt mit Gebraus, daß die Erde zitterte;

When the day dawned when the battle was to be fought, hu,
the four-footed beasts came running along with a roar that
made the earth tremble;

3.2 Zaunkönig mit seiner Armee kam auch durch die
Luft daher, die schnurrte, schrie und schwärmte, daß
einem angst und bange ward;

Wren and his army also came through the air, purring,
screaming, and swarming so that one was afraid;

3.3 und gingen sie da von beiden Seiten aneinander.

and they went at each other from both sides.

3.4 Der Zaunkönig aber schickte die Hornisse hinab, sie
sollte sich dem Fuchs unter den Schwanz setzen und
aus Leibeskräften stechen.

But the wren sent down the hornet to sit under the fox's tail
and sting with all her might.

3.5 Wie nun der Fuchs den ersten Stich bekam, zuckte
er, daß er das eine Bein aufhob, doch ertrug er's und
hielt den Schwanz noch in die Höhe:

When the fox received the first sting, he flinched so that he
lifted up one leg, but he endured it and still held up his tail:

3.6 beim zweiten Stich mußte er ihn einen Augenblick
herunterlassen;

at the second sting he had to let it down for a moment;

3.7 beim dritten aber konnte er sich nicht mehr halten,

but at the third he could hold himself no longer,

3.8 schrie und nahm den Schwanz zwischen die Beine.

screamed and took the tail between his legs.

Wie das die Tiere sahen, meinten sie, alles wäre   3.9
verloren und fingen an zu laufen, jeder in seine
Höhle, und hatten die Vögel die Schlacht gewonnen.
When the animals saw this, they thought all was lost and
began to run, each to his own cave, and the birds had won
the battle.

Da flog der Herr König und die Frau Königin heim zu   4.1
ihren Kindern und riefen:
Then the King and Queen flew home to their children and
cried,

»Kinder, seid fröhlich, eßt und trinkt nach   4.2
Herzenslust, wir haben den Krieg gewonnen.«
"Children, be merry, eat and drink to your heart's content,
we have won the war."

Die jungen Zaunkönige aber sagten: 4.3
But the young wrens said,

»Noch essen wir nicht, der Bär soll erst vor das Nest   4.4
kommen und Abbitte thun, und soll sagen, daß wir
ehrliche Kinder sind.«
"We will not eat yet; the bear must first come to the nest
and make amends, and say that we are honest children."

Da flog der Zaunkönig vor das Loch des Bären und   4.5
rief:
Then the wren flew before the bear's hole and cried,

»Brummbär, du sollst vor das Nest zu meinen   4.6
Kindern gehen und Abbitte thun und sagen, daß
sie ehrliche Kinder sind, sonst sollen dir die Rippen
im Leibe zertreten werden.«
"Grumpy bear, you must go before the nest to my children
and make amends and say that they are honest children,
otherwise your ribs shall be trampled underfoot."

4.7 **Da kroch der Bär in der größten Angst hin und that Abbitte.**

Then the bear crawled in great fear and made amends.

4.8 **Jetzt waren die jungen Zaunkönige erst zufrieden, setzten sich zusammen, aßen und tranken und machten sich lustig bis in die späte Nacht hinein.**

Now the young wrens were satisfied, sat down together, ate and drank, and made merry till late at night.

Der süße Brei

The Sweet Porridge

1.1 Es war einmal ein armes, frommes Mädchen, das lebte mit seiner Mutter allein, und sie hatten nichts mehr zu essen.

Once upon a time there was a poor, pious girl who lived alone with her mother, and they had nothing left to eat.

1.2 Da ging das Kind hinaus in den Wald und begegnete ihm da eine alte Frau, die wußte seinen Jammer schon und schenkte ihm ein Töpfchen, zu dem sollte es sagen,

So the child went out into the forest and met an old woman there, who knew of her misery and gave her a little pot, to which she was to say,

1.3 »Töpfchen, koche.«

"Pot, cook."

1.4 so kochte es guten, süßen Hirsebrei, und wenn es sagte,

so it cooked good, sweet millet porridge, and when she said,

1.5 »Töpfchen, steh.« so hörte es wieder auf zu kochen.

"Pot, stand." it stopped cooking again.

Das Mädchen brachte den Topf seiner Mutter heim,   1.6
The girl took the pot home to her mother,

und nun waren sie ihrer Armut und ihres Hungers   1.7
ledig und aßen süßen Brei so oft sie wollten.
and now they were free from poverty and hunger and ate
sweet porridge as often as they liked.

Auf eine Zeit war das Mädchen ausgegangen, da   1.8
sprach die Mutter,
After a time the girl had gone out, and her mother said,

»Töpfchen, koche.« da kochte es, und sie aß sich satt;   1.9
"Pot, boil." and it boiled, and she ate her fill;

nun will sie, daß das Töpfchen wieder aufhören soll,   1.10
aber sie weiß das Wort nicht.
now she wanted the pot to stop again, but she did not know
the word.

Also kochte es fort, und der Brei steigt über den Rand   1.11
hinaus und kocht immer zu, die Küche und das ganze
Haus voll, und das zweite Haus und dann die Straße,
als wollt's die ganze Welt satt machen, und ist die
größte Not, und kein Mensch weiß sich da zu helfen.
So it boiled away, and the porridge rose over the edge, and
boiled over and over, filling the kitchen and the whole
house, and the second house, and then the street, as if it
wanted to fill the whole world, and was the greatest trouble,
and no one knew how to help it.

Endlich, wie nur noch ein einziges Haus übrig ist, da   1.12
kommt das Kind heim und spricht nur:
At last, when there is only one house left, the child comes
home and says only,

»Töpfchen, steh.« da steht es und hört auf zu kochen;   1.13
"Potty, stand." and stands there and stops cooking;

1.14 **und wer wieder in die Stadt wollte, der mußte sich durchessen.**

and whoever wanted to go back to town had to eat his way through.

Die klugen Leute

The Clever People

1.1 Eines Tages holte ein Bauer seinen hagebüchenen
Stock aus der Ecke und sprach zu seiner Frau:
One day, a farmer took out his hay stick from the corner
and said to his wife:

1.2 »Trine,
"Trine,

1.3 ich gehe jetzt über Land und komme erst in drei
Tagen wieder zurück.
I'm going overland now and won't be back for three days.

1.4 Wenn der Viehhändler, in der Zeit bei uns einspricht
und will unsere drei Kühe kaufen, so kannst du sie
losschlagen, aber nicht anders als für zweihundert
Thaler, geringer nicht, hörst du.«
If the cattle dealer comes to us in that time and wants to
buy our three cows, you can get rid of them, but not for
anything other than two hundred thalers, no less, you
hear."

1.5 »Geh nur in Gottes Namen.« antwortete die Frau,
"Go ahead in God's name." replied the woman,

ich will das schon machen.«   1.6
"I'll do it."

»Ja, du!«   1.7
"Yes, you!"

sprach der Mann, du bist als ein kleines Kind einmal   1.8
auf den Kopf gefallen, das hängt dir bis auf diese
Stunde nach.
said the man, "you fell on your head once when you were a
little child, and you'll remember it to this hour.

Aber das sage ich dir, machst du dummes Zeug, so   1.9
streiche ich dir den Rücken blau an, und das ohne
Farbe, bloß mit dem Stock, den ich da in der Hand
habe, und der Anstrich soll ein ganzes Jahr halten,
darauf kannst du dich verlassen.«
But I'll tell you this, if you do anything stupid, I'll paint
your back blue, without paint, just with the stick I have in
my hand, and the paint will last a whole year, you can count
on that."

Damit ging der Mann seiner Wege.   1.10
With that, the man went his way.

Am anderen Morgen kam der Viehhändler,   2.1
The next morning the cattle dealer came,

und die Frau brauchte mit ihm nicht viel Worte zu   2.2
machen.
and the woman did not need to say much to him.

Als er die Kühe besehen hatte und den Preis vernahm,   2.3
sagte er,
When he had looked at the cows and heard the price, he
said,

2.4 »Das gebe ich gern,
"I'll gladly give that,

2.5 so viel sind sie unter Brüdern wert.
they're worth that much between brothers.

2.6 Ich will die Tiere gleich mitnehmen.«
I'll take the animals with me straight away."

2.7 Er machte sie von der Kette los und trieb sie aus dem Stall.
He unchained them and drove them out of the stable.

2.8 Als er eben zum Hofthor hinauswollte, faßte ihn die Frau am Ärmel und sprach,
As he was about to leave the yard gate, the woman grabbed him by the sleeve and said,

2.9 »Ihr müßt mir erst die zweihundert Thaler geben,
"You must give me the two hundred thalers first,

2.10 sonst kann ich Euch nicht gehen lassen.«
otherwise I can't let you go."

2.11 »Richtig.« antwortete der Mann,
"That's right." replied the man,

2.12 »ich habe nur vergessen, meine Geldkatze umzuschnallen.
"I just forgot to put my money belt on.

2.13 Aber macht Euch keine Sorge, Ihr sollt Sicherheit haben, bis ich zahle.
But don't worry, you shall be safe until I pay.

Zwei Kühe nehme ich mit und die dritte lasse ich Euch zurück,   2.14

I'll take two cows with me and leave you the third,

so habt Ihr ein gutes Pfand.« Der Frau leuchtete das ein,   2.15

so you'll have a good deposit." This made sense to the woman,

sie ließ den Mann mit seinen Kühen abziehen und dachte: 2.16

she let the man leave with his cows and thought:

»Wie wird sich der Hans freuen, wenn er sieht, daß ich es so klug gemacht habe.«   2.17

"How Hans will be pleased when he sees that I have done it so wisely."

Der Bauer kam den dritten Tag, wie er gesagt hatte, nach Hause und fragte gleich, ob die Kühe verkauft wären.   2.18

The farmer came home the third day, as he had said, and immediately asked if the cows had been sold.

»Freilich, lieber Hans.«   2.19

"Of course, dear Hans."

antwortete die Frau, und wie du gesagt hast, für zweihundert Thaler.   2.20

replied the woman, "and as you said, for two hundred thalers.

So viel sind sie kaum wert,   2.21

They are hardly worth that much,

aber der Mann nahm sie ohne Widerrede.«   2.22

but the man took them without argument."

2.23 »Wo ist das Geld?« fragte der Bauer.
"Where is the money?" asked the farmer.

2.24 »Das Geld das habe ich nicht.« antwortete die Frau,
"I haven't got the money." answered the woman;

2.25 »er hatte gerade seine Geldkatze vergessen,
"he had just forgotten his money-cat,

2.26 wird's aber bald bringen;
but he will soon bring it;

2.27 er hat mir ein gutes Pfand zurückgelassen.«
he has left me a good pledge."

2.28 »Was für ein Pfand?« fragte der Mann.
"What kind of pledge?" asked the man.

2.29 »Eine von den drei Kühen, die kriegt er nicht eher, als bis er die anderen bezahlt hat.
"One of the three cows, he won't get it until he's paid for the others.

2.30 Ich habe es klug gemacht, ich habe die kleinste zurückbehalten, die frißt am wenigsten.«
I did it wisely, I kept the smallest one, it eats the least."

2.31 Der Mann ward zornig,
The man became angry,

2.32 hob seinen Stock in die Höhe und wollte ihr damit den verheißenen Anstrich geben.
raised his stick in the air and wanted to give her the promised touch.

2.33 Plötzlich ließ er ihn sinken und sagte:
Suddenly he lowered it and said,

»Du bist die dümmste Gans, die auf Gottes Erdboden herumwackelt, aber du dauerst mich. 2.34

"You are the stupidest goose wobbling around on God's earth, but you are keeping me.

Ich will auf die Landstraße gehen und drei Tage lang warten, ob ich jemand finde, der noch einfältiger ist als du bist. 2.35

I will go out into the country and wait three days to see if I can find someone even more stupid than you.

Glückt mir's, so sollst du frei sein, finde ich ihn aber nicht, so sollst du deinen wohlverdienten Lohn ohne Abzug erhalten.« 2.36

If I succeed, you shall be free, but if I don't find him, you shall receive your well-earned wages without deduction."

Er ging hinaus auf die große Straße, setzte sich auf einen Stein und wartete auf die Dinge, die da kommen sollten. 3.1

He went out onto the big road, sat down on a stone and waited for what was to come.

Da sah er einen Leiterwagen heranfahren, und eine Frau stand mitten darauf, statt auf dem Gebund Stroh zu sitzen, das dabei lag, oder neben den Ochsen zu gehen und sie zu leiten. 3.2

Then he saw a cart approaching, and a woman was standing in the middle of it, instead of sitting on the bundle of straw that lay beside it, or walking beside the oxen and leading them.

Der Mann dachte, 3.3

The man thought,

»Das ist wohl eine, wie du sie suchst.« 3.4

"That's probably the kind of woman you're looking for."

3.5 sprang auf und lief vor dem Wagen hin und her wie einer, der nicht recht gescheit ist.

and jumped up and ran back and forth in front of the cart like someone who is not very clever.

3.6 »Was wollt Ihr, Gevatter.« sagte die Frau zu ihm,

"What do you want, father." said the woman to him,

3.7 »ich kenne Euch nicht, von wo kommt Ihr her?«

"I don't know you, where do you come from?"

3.8 Ich bin von dem Himmel gefallen.« antwortete der Mann,

I have fallen from heaven." answered the man,

3.9 »und weiß nicht wie ich wieder hin kommen soll;

"and do not know how to get back again;

3.10 könnt Ihr mich nicht hinauffahren?«

can you not drive me up?"

3.11 »Nein.« sagte die Frau, »ich weiß den Weg nicht.

"No." said the woman, "I don't know the way.

3.12 Aber wenn Ihr aus dem Himmel kommt, so könnt Ihr mir wohl sagen, wie es meinem Mann geht, der schon seit drei Jahren dort ist:

But if you have come from heaven, you can tell me how my husband is, who has been there for three years:

3.13 Ihr habt ihn gewiß gesehen?«

Surely you have seen him?"

3.14 »Ich habe ihn wohl gesehen,

"I have seen him,

61

aber es kann nicht allen Menschen gut gehen.   3.15
but not all men can be well.

Er hütet die Schafe, und das liebe Vieh macht ihm   3.16
viel zu schaffen, das springt auf die Berge und verirrt
sich in der Wildnis, und da muß er hinterherlaufen
und es wieder zusammentreiben.
He tends the sheep, and the cattle give him a lot of trouble,
they jump up the mountains and get lost in the wilderness,
and he has to run after them and round them up again.

Abgerissen ist er auch,   3.17
He is also torn,

und die Kleider werden ihm bald vom Leibe fallen.   3.18
and his clothes will soon fall off his body.

Schneider giebt dort nicht, der heil. Petrus läßt   3.19
keinen hinein, wie Ihr aus dem Märchen wißt.«
There are no tailors there, St. Peter won't let anyone in, as
you know from the fairy tale."

»Wer hätte sich das gedacht!« rief die Frau,   3.20
"Who would have thought it!" cried the woman,

»wißt Ihr was?   3.21
"do you know what?

Ich will seinen Sonntagsrock holen, der noch daheim   3.22
im Schrank hängt, den kann er dort mit Ehren
tragen.
I want to get his Sunday coat, which is still hanging in the
closet at home, so he can wear it there with honor.

Ihr seid so gut und nehmt ihn mit.«   3.23
You'll be good enough to take it with you."

3.24 »Das geht nicht wohl.« antwortete der Bauer.
"That won't do." replied the farmer.

3.25 Kleider darf man nicht in den Himmel bringen,
You can't take clothes to heaven,

3.26 die werden einem vor dem Thor abgenommen.«
they'll be taken from you at the gate."

3.27 »Hört mich an.« sprach die Frau,
"Listen to me." said the woman,

3.28 »ich habe gestern meinen schönen Weizen verkauft und ein hübsches Geld dafür bekommen, das will ich ihm schicken.
"I sold my fine wheat yesterday, and got a handsome sum of money for it, which I will send him.

3.29 Wenn Ihr den Beutel in die Tasche steckt,
If you put the bag in your pocket,

3.30 so wird's kein Mensch gewahr.«
no one will notice it."

3.31 »Kann's nicht anders sein.« erwiderte der Bauer,
"It can't be otherwise." replied the farmer,

3.32 »so will ich Euch wohl den Gefallen thun.«
"so I will do you the favor."

3.33 »Bleibt nur dasitzen.« sagte sie,
"Just sit there." she said,

3.34 »ich will heimfahren und den Beutel holen;
"I want to go home and fetch the bag;

3.35 ich bin bald wieder hier.
I'll be back soon.

Ich setze mich nicht auf das Bund Stroh, sondern stehe auf dem Wagen, so hat's das Vieh leichter.«

3.36

I won't sit on the bundle of straw, but stand on the cart, so it's easier for the cattle."

Sie trieb ihre Ochsen an, und der Bauer dachte:

3.37

She drove her oxen, and the farmer thought:

»Die hat Anlage zur Narrheit, bringt sie das Geld wirklich, so kann meine Frau von Glück sagen, denn sie kriegt keine Schläge.«

3.38

"She's a fool; if she really brings the money, my wife can count herself lucky, because she won't get a beating."

Es dauerte nicht lange, so kam sie gelaufen, brachte das Geld und steckte es ihm selbst in die Tasche.

3.39

It wasn't long before she came running, brought the money and put it in his pocket herself.

Ehe sie wegging,

3.40

Before she left,

dankte sie ihm noch tausendmal für seine Gefälligkeit.

3.41

she thanked him a thousand times for his kindness.

Als die Frau wieder heimkam, so fand sie ihren Sohn, der aus dem Felde zurückgekehrt war.

4.1

When the woman returned home, she found her son, who had returned from the field.

Sie erzählte ihm, was sie für unerwartete Dinge erfahren hätte und setzte dann hinzu:

4.2

She told him what unexpected things she had learned and then added:

4.3 »Ich freue mich recht, daß ich Gelegenheit gefunden habe, meinem armem Mann etwas zu schicken, wer hätte sich vorgestellt, daß er im Himmel an etwas Mangel leiden würde?«

"I am very glad that I have found an opportunity to send something to my poor husband, who would have imagined that he would be in want of anything in heaven?"

4.4 Der Sohn war in der größten Verwunderung. »Mutter.«

The son was in the greatest astonishment. "Mother."

4.5 sagte er,

said he,

4.6 »so einer aus dem Himmel kommt nicht alle Tage, ich will gleich hinaus und sehen, daß ich den Mann noch finde: der muß mir erzählen, wie's dort aussieht und wie's mit der Arbeit geht.«

"such a man does not come from heaven every day; I will go out at once and see if I can find him; he must tell me how things are there, and how the work is going on."

4.7 Er sattelte das Pferd und ritt in aller Hast fort.

He saddled the horse and rode off in a hurry.

4.8 Er fand den Bauer, der unter einem Weidenbaum saß und das Geld, das im Beutel war, zählen wollte.

He found the farmer sitting under a willow tree and counting the money in his pouch.

4.9 »Habt Ihr nicht den Mann gesehen.« rief ihm der Junge zu,

"Didn't you see the man." the boy called to him,

4.10 »der aus dem Himmel gekommen ist?«

"who has come down from heaven?"

»Ja.« antwortete der Bauer,   4.11
"Yes." replied the farmer,

»der hat sich wieder auf den Rückweg gemacht und   4.12
ist den Berg dort hinauf gegangen, von wo er's etwas
näher hat.
"he has set off on his way back and gone up the mountain
from where he is a little closer.

Ihr könnt ihn noch einholen, wenn Ihr scharf reitet.«   4.13
You can still catch up with him if you ride hard."

»Ach.« sagte der Junge,   4.14
"Oh." said the boy,

»ich habe mich den ganzen Tag abgeäschert und der   4.15
Ritt hierher hat mich vollends müde gemacht:
"I've been washing all day and the ride here has made me
completely tired:

Ihr kennt den Mann, seid so gut und setzt Euch   4.16
auf mein Pferd und überredet ihn, daß er hierher
kommt.«
You know the man, be good enough to sit on my horse and
persuade him to come here."

»Aha.« meinte der Bauer,   4.17
"I see." said the farmer,

»das ist auch einer, der keinen Docht in seiner Lampe   4.18
hat.«
"that's another one who has no wick in his lamp."

»Warum sollte ich Euch den Gefallen nicht thun?«   4.19
sprach er,
"Why should I not do you the favor?" said he,

4.20 stieg auf und ritt im stärksten Trabe fort.

mounting and riding away at a brisk trot.

4.21 Der Junge blieb sitzen, bis die Nacht einbrach, aber der Bauer kam nicht zurück.

The boy remained seated until nightfall, but the farmer did not return.

4.22 »Gewiß.« dachte er,

"Surely." he thought,

4.23 »hat der Mann aus dem Himmel große Eile gehabt und nicht umkehren wollen, und der Bauer hat ihm das Pferd mitgegeben, um es meinem Vater zu bringen.«

"the man from heaven was in a great hurry and did not want to turn back, and the farmer gave him the horse to bring to my father."

4.24 Er ging heim und erzählte seiner Mutter was geschehen war:

He went home and told his mother what had happened:

4.25 das Pferd habe er dem Vater geschickt, damit er nicht immer herumzulaufen brauche.

he had sent the horse to his father so that he wouldn't always have to walk around.

4.26 »Du hast wohlgethan.« antwortete sie,

"You have done well." she replied,

4.27 »du hast noch junge Beine und kannst zu Fuß gehen.«

"you still have young legs and can walk."

Als der Bauer nach Hause gekommen war, stellte er 5.1
das Pferd in den Stall neben die verpfändete Kuh,
ging dann zu seiner Frau und sagte:
When the farmer got home, he put the horse in the stable
next to the pawned cow, then went to his wife and said,

»Trine, das war dein Glück, ich habe zwei gefunden, 5.2
die noch einfältigere Narren sind als du:
"Trine, that was your luck, I've found two even more
simple-minded fools than you:

diesmal kommst du ohne Schläge davon, 5.3
this time you'll get away without a beating,

ich will sie für eine andere Gelegenheit aufsparen.« 5.4
I'll save them for another occasion."

Dann zündete er seine Pfeife an, setzte sich in den 5.5
Großvaterstuhl und sprach,
Then he lit his pipe, sat down in his grandfather's chair and
said,

»Das war ein gutes Geschäft, 5.6
"That was a good bargain,

für zwei magere Kühe ein glattes Pferd und dazu 5.7
einen großen Beutel voll Geld.
for two lean cows a smooth horse and a big bag of money to
boot.

Wenn die Dummheit immer so viel einbrächte, 5.8
If stupidity always brought in so much,

so wollte ich sie gern in Ehren halten.« So dachte der 5.9
Bauer,
I would like to keep it in honor." So thought the farmer,

5.10 **aber dir sind gewiß die einfältigen lieber.**
but you certainly prefer the simple-minded.

Märchen von der Unke

Fairy Tale of the Toad

— I —

2.1 **Es war einmal ein kleines Kind, dem gab seine Mutter jeden Nachmittag ein Schüsselchen mit Milch und Weckbrocken, und das Kind setzte sich damit hinaus in den Hof.**

Once upon a time, there was a small child whose mother gave him a bowl of milk and a lump of bread every afternoon, and the child sat out in the yard with it.

2.2 **Wenn es aber anfing zu essen, so kam die Hausunke aus einer Mauerritze hervorgekrochen, senkte ihr Köpfchen in die Milch und aß mit.**

But when he started to eat, the house toad crawled out of a crack in the wall, lowered its head into the milk and ate with him.

2.3 **Das Kind hatte seine Freude daran, und wenn es mit seinem Schüsselchen dasaß und die Unke kam nicht gleich herbei, so rief es ihr zu:**

The child enjoyed it, and if he sat there with his bowl and the toad didn't come straight away, he would call out to it:

71

»Unke, Unke, komm geschwind,

"Unke, Unke, come quickly,

komm herbei, du kleines Ding,

Come here, you little thing,

sollst dein Bröckchen haben,

shall have your crumb,

an der Milch dich laben.«

feast on the milk."

Da kam die Unke gelaufen und ließ es sich gut schmecken.

4.1

Then the toad came running and had a good time.

Sie zeigte sich auch dankbar, denn sie brachte dem Kinde aus ihrem heimlichen Schatz allerlei schöne Dinge, glänzende Steine, Perlen und goldene Spielsachen.

4.2

He was also grateful, because he brought the child all kinds of beautiful things from his secret treasure, shiny stones, pearls and golden toys.

Die Unke trank aber nur Milch und ließ die Brocken liegen.

4.3

But the toad only drank milk and left the lumps lying around.

Da nahm das Kind einmal sein Löffelchen, schlug ihr damit sanft auf den Kopf und sagte,

4.4

Once the child took his spoon, hit her gently on the head with it and said,

»Ding, iß auch Brocken.«

4.5

"Ding, eat some chunks too."

4.6 Die Mutter, die in der Küche stand, hörte, daß das Kind mit jemand sprach, und als sie sah, daß es mit seinem Löffelchen nach einer Unke schlug, so lief sie mit einem Scheit Holz heraus und tötete das gute Tier.

The mother, who was standing in the kitchen, heard that the child was talking to someone, and when she saw that he was hitting a toad with his spoon, she ran out with a log of wood and killed the good animal.

5.1 Von der Zeit an ging eine Veränderung mit dem Kinde vor.

From that time on, a change took place in the child.

5.2 Es war, so lange die Unke mit ihm gegessen hatte, groß und stark geworden, jetzt aber verlor es seine schönen roten Backen und magerte ab.

He had grown big and strong as long as the toad had eaten with him, but now he lost his beautiful red cheeks and grew thin.

5.3 Nicht lange, so fing in der Nacht der Totenvogel an zu schreien, und das Rotkehlchen sammelte Zweiglein und Blätter zu einem Totenkranz, und bald hernach lag das Kind auf der Bahre.

It was not long before the bird of death began to cry in the night, and the robin gathered twigs and leaves to make a funeral wreath, and soon afterward the child lay on the bier.

— II —

Ein Waisenkind saß an der Stadtmauer und spann, 7.1
da sah es eine Unke aus einer Öffnung unten an der
Mauer hervorkommen.

An orphan was sitting on the city wall, stretching, when
he saw a toad emerge from an opening at the bottom of the
wall.

Geschwind breitete es sein blauseidenes Halstuch 7.2
neben sich aus,

He quickly spread out his blue silk scarf next to him,

das die Unken gewaltig lieben und auf das sie allein 7.3
gehen.

which the toads love very much and which they go to alone.

Sobald die Unke das erblickte, kehrte sie um, kam 7.4
wieder und brachte ein kleines goldenes Krönchen
getragen, legte es darauf und ging dann wieder fort.

As soon as the toad saw this, she turned back, came again
carrying a little golden crown, placed it on her head and
then went away again.

Das Mädchen nahm die Krone auf, 7.5

The girl picked up the crown,

sie glitzerte und war von zartem Goldgespinst. 7.6

it glittered and was made of delicate gold thread.

7.7 Nicht lange, so kam die Unke zum zweitenmal wieder: wie sie aber die Krone nicht mehr sah, kroch sie an die Wand und schlug vor Leid ihr Köpfchen so lange dawider, als sie nur noch Kräfte hatte, bis sie endlich tot da lag.

It was not long before the toad came again for the second time, but when she no longer saw the crown, she crawled up against the wall and banged her head against it in sorrow for as long as she had strength left, until at last she lay there dead.

7.8 Hätte das Mädchen die Krone liegen lassen,

If the girl had left the crown lying there,

7.9 die Unke hätte wohl noch mehr von ihren Schätzen aus der Höhle herbeigetragen.

the toad would probably have carried more of her treasures out of the cave.

— III —

9.1 Unke ruft: »Huhu, huhu.« Kind spricht:

Toad calls: "Woo-hoo, woo-hoo." Child says:

9.2 »Komm herut.«

"Come here."

9.3 Die Unke kommt hervor, da fragt das Kind nach seinem Schwesterchen:

The toad comes out and the child asks about his little sister:

9.4 »Hast du Rotstrümpfchen nicht gesehen?« Unke sagt: »Ne,

"Haven't you seen Little Red Trumpet?" Unke says: "No,

ik og nit: wie du denn? huhu, huhu, huhu.«

9.5

I haven't: how did you? huhu, huhu, huhu."

Der arme Müllerbursch und das Kätzchen

The Poor Miller's Boy and the Kitten

1.1 In einer Mühle lebte ein alter Müller, der hatte weder Frau noch Kinder, und drei Müllerburschen dienten bei ihm.
There lived an old miller in a mill who had neither wife nor children, and three miller's boys served him.

1.2 Wie sie nun etliche Jahre bei ihm gewesen waren,
After they had been with him for several years,

1.3 sagte er eines Tages zu ihnen:
he said to them one day:

1.4 »Ich bin alt und will mich hinter den Ofen setzen;
"I am old and want to sit behind the stove;

1.5 zieht aus und wer mir das beste Pferd nach Hause bringt,
go out and whoever brings me the best horse home,

dem will ich die Mühle geben und er soll mich dafür
bis an meinen Tod verpflegen.« 1.6

I will give him the mill and he shall feed me for it until I
die."

Der dritte von den Burschen war aber der
Kleinknecht, der ward von den anderen für albern
gehalten, dem gönnten sie die Mühle nicht: und er
wollte sie hernach nicht einmal. 1.7

But the third of the lads was the little servant, who was
considered foolish by the others, they did not grant him the
mill, and he did not even want it afterwards.

Da zogen sie alle drei miteinander aus, und wie sie
vor das Dorf kamen, sagten die zwei zu dem albernen
Hans, 1.8

So they all three went out together, and when they came to
the village, the two said to silly Hans,

»Du kannst nur hier bleiben, 1.9

"You can only stay here,

du kriegst dein Lebtag keinen Gaul.« 1.10

you won't get a horse for the rest of your life."

Hans aber ging doch mit, und als es Nacht war,
kamen sie an eine Höhle, da hinein legten sie sich
schlafen. 1.11

But Hans went with them, and when night fell, they came
to a cave and went to sleep in it.

1.12 Die zwei Klugen warteten, bis Hans eingeschlafen war, dann stiegen sie auf, machten sich fort und ließen Hänschen liegen, und meinten's recht sein gemacht zu haben Ja, es wird euch doch nicht gut gehen!

The two clever men waited until Hans had fallen asleep, then they got up, went away and left Hans lying there, and thought they had done well, yes, you will not do well after all!

1.13 Wie nun die Sonne kam und Hans aufwachte,

When the sun came out and Hans woke up,

1.14 lag er in einer tiefen Höhle;

he was lying in a deep cave;

1.15 er guckte sich überall um und rief: »Ach Gott,

he looked around everywhere and cried: "Oh God,

1.16 wo bin ich!« Da erhob er sich und krabbelte die Höhle hinauf,

where am I!" Then he got up and crawled up the cave,

1.17 ging in den Wald und dachte:

went into the forest and thought:

1.18 »Ich bin hier ganz allein und verlassen,

"I'm all alone and deserted here,

1.19 wie soll ich nun zu einem Pferde kommen!«

how am I going to get to a horse!"

1.20 Indem er so in Gedanken dahinging, begegnete ihm ein kleines buntes Kätzchen, das sprach ganz freundlich:

As he was walking along in his thoughts, he met a little colorful kitten who said in a very friendly way:

79

»Hans, wo willst du hin!«   1.21
"Hans, where are you going!"

»Ach, du kannst mir doch nicht helfen.«   1.22
"Oh, you can't help me."

»Was dein Begehren ist, weiß ich wohl.« sprach das   1.23
Kätzchen,
"I know what you want." said the kitten,

»du willst einen hübschen Gaul haben.   1.24
"you want a pretty horse.

Komm mit mir und sei sieben Jahre lang mein treuer   1.25
Knecht, so will ich dir einen geben, schöner als du
dein Lebtag einen gesehen hast.«
Come with me and be my faithful servant for seven years,
and I will give you one more beautiful than you have ever
seen in your life."

»Nun, das ist eine wunderliche Katze.« dachte Hans,   1.26
"Well, that's a strange cat." thought Hans,

»aber sehen will ich doch, ob das wahr ist was sie   1.27
sagt.«
"but I want to see if what she says is true."

Da nahm sie ihn mit in ihr verwünschtes Schlößchen   1.28
und hatte da lauter Kätzchen, die ihr dienten:
So she took him into her cursed little castle and had a lot of
kittens there to serve her:

die sprangen flink die Treppe auf und ab,   1.29
they jumped nimbly up and down the stairs,

waren lustig und guter Dinge.   1.30
were merry and in good spirits.

1.31 Abends, als sie sich zu Tisch setzten, mußten drei Musik machen:

In the evening, when they sat down to dinner, three of them had to make music:

1.32 eins strich den Baß, das andere die Geige, das dritte setzte die Trompete an und blies die Backen auf, so sehr es nur konnte.

one played the bass, the other the violin, the third played the trumpet and blew its cheeks as hard as it could.

1.33 Als sie gegessen hatten, wurde der Tisch weggetragen, und die Katze sagte,

When they had eaten, the table was carried away, and the cat said,

1.34 »Nun komm, Hans, und tanze mit mir.«

"Now come, Hans, and dance with me."

1.35 »Nein.« antwortete er,

"No." he replied,

1.36 »mit einer Miezekatze tanze ich nicht,

"I won't dance with a pussycat,

1.37 das habe ich noch niemals gethan.«

I've never done that before."

1.38 »So bringt ihn ins Bett.« sagte sie zu den Kätzchen.

"Put him to bed." she said to the kittens.

1.39 Da leuchtete ihm eins in seine Schlafkammer, eins zog ihm die Schuhe aus, eins die Strümpfe und zuletzt blies eins das Licht aus.

So one of them shone the light into his bedchamber, one took off his shoes, one took off his stockings, and finally one blew out the light.

Am anderen Morgen kamen sie wieder und halfen ihm aus dem Bett:

1.40

The next morning they came again and helped him out of bed:

eins zog ihm die Strümpfe an, eins band ihm die Strumpfbänder, eins holte die Schuhe, eins wusch ihn und eins trocknete ihm mit dem Schwanz das Gesicht ab.

1.41

one put on his stockings, one tied his garters, one fetched his shoes, one washed him and one dried his face with its tail.

»Das thut recht sanft.« sagte Hans.

1.42

"That's very gentle." said Hans.

Er mußte aber auch der Katze dienen und alle Tage Holz klein machen;

1.43

But he also had to serve the cat, and chop wood every day;

dazu kriegte er eine Axt von Silber, und die Keile und Säge von Silber, und der Schläger war von Kupfer.

1.44

for this he was given an axe of silver, and the wedges and saw of silver, and the mallet was of copper.

Nun, da machte er's klein, blieb da im Haus, hatte sein gutes Essen und Trinken, sah aber niemand als die bunte Katze und ihr Gesinde.

1.45

So he made it small, stayed there in the house, had his good food and drink, but saw no one but the colorful cat and her servants.

Einmal sagte sie zu ihm: »Geh hin und mähe meine Wiese,

1.46

Once she said to him, "Go and mow my meadow,

und mache das Gras trocken.«

1.47

and make the grass dry."

1.48 und gab ihm von Silber eine Sense und von Gold einen Wetzstein,

and gave him a scythe of silver and a whetstone of gold,

1.49 hieß ihn aber auch alles wieder richtig abliefern.

but told him to deliver everything properly.

1.50 Da ging Hans hin und that was ihm geheißen war; nach vollbrachter Arbeit trug er Sense, Wetzstein und Heu nach Hause, und fragte, ob sie ihm noch nicht seinen Lohn geben wollte.

So Hans went and did as he was told, and when he had finished his work, he carried the scythe, whetstone and hay home, and asked if she would not yet give him his wages.

1.51 »Nein.« sagte die Katze,

"No." said the cat,

1.52 »du sollst mir erst noch einerlei thun, da ist Bauholz von Silber, Zimmeraxt, Winkeleisen und was nötig ist, alles von Silber, daraus baue mir erst ein kleines Häuschen.«

"you shall do me one thing first, there is timber of silver, a carpenter's axe, angle-iron, and what is necessary, all of silver, from which I shall first build a little house."

1.53 Da baute Hans das Häuschen fertig und sagte, er hätte nun alles gethan, und hätte noch kein Pferd.

So Hans finished building the little house and said that he had now done everything and still had no horse.

1.54 Doch waren ihm die sieben Jahre herumgegangen wie ein halbes.

But the seven years had gone by like half a year.

1.55 Fragte die Katze, ob er ihre Pferde sehen wollte? »Ja.«

Did the cat ask if he wanted to see her horses? "Yes."

sagte Hans.   1.56

said Hans.

Da machte sie ihm das Häuschen auf, und weil sie   1.57
die Thür so aufmacht, da stehen zwölf Pferde, ach,
die waren gewesen ganz stolz, die hatten geblänkt
und gespiegelt, daß sich sein Herz im Leibe darüber
freute.

Then she opened the little house to him, and as she opened
the door, there were twelve horses, oh, they had been so
proud, they had barked and reflected so that his heart
rejoiced in his body.

Nun gab sie ihm zu essen, und zu trinken und sprach: 1.58

Then she gave him something to eat and drink, and said,

»Geh heim, dein Pferd gebe ich dir nicht mit: in drei   1.59
Tagen aber komm ich und bringe dir's nach.«

"Go home, I will not give you your horse, but I will come in
three days and bring it to you."

Also machte Hans sich auf und sie zeigte ihm den   1.60
Weg zur Mühle.

So Hans set off and she showed him the way to the mill.

Sie hatte ihm aber nicht einmal ein neues Kleid   1.61
gegeben, sondern er mußte sein altes lumpiges
Kittelchen behalten, das er mitgebracht hatte,
und das ihm in den sieben Jahren überall zu kurz
geworden war.

But she had not even given him a new dress, but he had to
keep his old ragged smock, which he had brought with him,
and which had become too short for him in seven years.

Wie er nun heimkam,   1.62

When he came home,

84

1.63 so waren die beiden anderen Müllerburschen auch wieder da:

the two other miller's boys were there again:

1.64 jeder hatte zwar sein Pferd mitgebracht, aber des einen seins war blind, des anderen seins lahm.

each had brought his horse with him, but one of them was blind and the other lame.

1.65 Sie fragten: »Hans, wo hast du dein Pferd?«

They asked: "Hans, where's your horse?"

1.66 »In drei Tagen wird's nachkommen.« Da lachten sie und sagten:

"He'll be here in three days." Then they laughed and said,

1.67 »Ja du, Hans, wo willst du ein Pferd herkriegen, das wird was Rechtes sein!«

"Yes, Hans, where are you going to get a horse, it will be something right!"

1.68 Hans ging in die Stube, der Müller sagte aber, er sollte nicht an den Tisch kommen, er wäre so zerrissen und zerlumpt, man müßte sich schämen, wenn jemand hereinkäme.

Hans went into the parlor, but the miller said he should not come to the table, he was so torn and ragged that he would be ashamed if anyone came in.

1.69 Da gaben sie ihm ein bißchen Essen hinaus, und wie sie abends schlafen gingen, wollten ihm die zwei anderen kein Bett geben, und er mußte endlich ins Gänseställchen kriechen und sich auf ein wenig hartes Stroh legen.

So they gave him a little food, and when they went to bed in the evening, the two others would not give him a bed, and at last he had to crawl into the goose-house and lie down on a little hard straw.

Am Morgen, wie er aufwacht, sind schon die drei 1.70
Tage herum, und es kommt eine Kutsche mit sechs
Pferden, ei, die glänzten, daß es schön war, und ein
Bedienter, der brachte noch ein siebentes, das war
für den armen Müllerburschen.

In the morning, when he awoke, three days had already
passed, and a carriage came with six horses, ei, they shone
so beautifully, and a servant who brought a seventh, which
was for the poor miller's boy.

Aus der Kutsche aber stieg eine prächtige 1.71
Königstochter und ging in die Mühle hinein, und
die Königstochter war das kleine bunte Kätzchen,
dem der arme Hans sieben Jahre gedient hatte.

But a splendid king's daughter got out of the carriage and
went into the mill, and the king's daughter was the little
colorful kitten whom poor Hans had served for seven years.

Sie fragte den Müller, wo der Mahlbursch, der 1.72
Kleinknecht wäre?

She asked the miller where the grinder's boy, the little
servant, was?

Da sagte der Müller: »Den können wir nicht in die 1.73
Mühle nehmen,

The miller said, "We can't take him into the mill,

der ist so verrissen und liegt im Gänsestall.« 1.74

he's so torn up and is lying in the goose house."

Da sagte die Königstochter, sie sollten ihn gleich 1.75
holen.

Then the king's daughter said they should fetch him
straight away.

86

1.76 Also holten sie ihn heraus, und er mußte sein Kittelchen zusammenpacken, um sich zu bedecken.

So they took him out and he had to pack up his smock to cover himself.

1.77 Da schnallte der Bediente prächtige Kleider aus und mußte ihn waschen und anziehen, und wie er fertig war, konnte kein König schöner aussehen.

Then the servant unbuckled splendid clothes, and had to wash and dress him, and when he was ready, no king could look more beautiful.

1.78 Danach verlangte die Jungfrau die Pferde zu sehen, welche die anderen Mahlburschen mitgebracht hatten, eins war blind, das andere lahm.

Then the maiden asked to see the horses which the other menservants had brought with them, one was blind and the other lame.

1.79 Da ließ sie den Bedienten das siebente Pferd bringen; wie der Müller das sah, sprach er, so eins wäre ihm noch nicht auf den Hof gekommen,

Then she had the servant bring the seventh horse, and when the miller saw it, he said that such a horse had not yet come into his court,

1.80 »und das ist für den dritten Mahlburschen.« sagte sie.

"and this is for the third grinder." said she.

1.81 »Da muß er die Mühle haben.«

"He must have the mill."

sagte der Müller; die Königstochter aber sprach, da wäre das Pferd, er sollte seine Mühle auch behalten; und nimmt ihren treuen Hans und setzt ihn in die Kutsche und fährt mit ihm fort. 1.82

said the miller; but the king's daughter said that there was the horse, and that he should keep his mill too, and she took her faithful Hans and put him into the carriage and drove away with him.

Sie fahren zuerst nach dem kleinen Häuschen, das er mit dem silbernen Werkzeug gebaut hat, da ist es ein großes Schloß, und ist alles darin von Silber und Gold; 1.83

They go first to the little house which he had built with the silver tools, and there it is a great castle, and everything in it is of silver and gold;

und da hat sie ihn geheiratet, und war er reich, so reich, daß er für sein Lebtag genug hatte. 1.84

and there she married him, and he was rich, so rich that he had enough for his lifetime.

Darum soll keiner sagen, daß wer albern ist, deshalb nichts Rechtes werden könne. 1.85

Therefore let no one say that he who is foolish can therefore become nothing right.

Die beiden Wanderer

The Two Hikers

1.1 **Berg und Thal begegnen sich nicht, wohl aber die Menschenkinder, zumal gute und böse.**

Mountain and valley do not meet, but the children of men do, especially the good and the bad.

1.2 **So kam auch einmal ein Schuster und ein Schneider auf der Wanderschaft zusammen.**

Once upon a time, a shoemaker and a tailor came together on their travels.

1.3 **Der Schneider war ein kleiner, hübscher Kerl und war immer lustig und guter Dinge.**

The tailor was a handsome little fellow and was always cheerful and in good spirits.

1.4 **Er sah den Schuster von der anderen Seite herankommen, und da er an seinem Felleisen merkte, was er für ein Handwerk trieb, rief er ihm ein Spottliedchen zu:**

He saw the shoemaker approaching from the other side, and when he realized by his hides what kind of work he was doing, he called out a mocking song to him:

»Nähe mir die Naht,

"Sew me the seam,

ziehe mir den Draht,

pull the wire,

streich ihn rechts und links mit Pech,

paint it right and left with pitch,

schlag, schlag mir fest den Zweck.«

hit me, hit me hard for the purpose."

Der Schuster aber konnte keinen Spaß vertragen, er verzog das Gesicht, als wenn er Essig getrunken hätte, und machte Miene, das Schneiderlein am Kragen zu packen. 3.1

But the cobbler couldn't take a joke, he grimaced as if he had been drinking vinegar and made a face to grab the little tailor by the collar.

Der kleine Kerl fing aber an zu lachen, reichte ihm seine Flasche und sprach, 3.2

But the little fellow began to laugh, handed him his bottle and said,

»Es ist nicht bös gemeint, 3.3

"I don't mean any harm,

trink einmal und schluck die Galle hinunter.« 3.4

drink once and swallow the bile."

Der Schuster that einen gewaltigen Schluck, und das Gewitter auf seinem Gesicht fing an zu verziehen. 3.5

The cobbler took a huge gulp and the storm on his face began to fade.

Er gab dem Schneider die Flasche zurück und sprach: 3.6

He gave the bottle back to the tailor and said,

90

3.7 »Ich habe ihr ordentlich zugesprochen, man sagt wohl vom vielen Trinken, aber nicht vom großen Durst.

"I've given her a good drink, they say from drinking a lot, but not from being very thirsty.

3.8 Wollen wir zusammen wandern?«

Shall we walk together?"

3.9 »Mir ist's recht.« antwortete der Schneider,

"That's fine with me." replied the tailor,

3.10 »wenn du nur Lust hast in eine große Stadt zu gehen, wo es nicht an Arbeit fehlt.«

"if only you feel like going to a big city where there's no shortage of work."

3.11 »Gerade dahin wollte ich auch.« antwortete der Schuster,

"That's exactly where I want to go." replied the shoemaker,

3.12 »in einem kleinen Nest ist nichts zu verdienen,

"there's nothing to earn in a small town,

3.13 und auf dem Lande gehen die Leute lieber barfuß.«

and people prefer to go barefoot in the country."

3.14 Sie wanderten also zusammen weiter und setzten immer einen Fuß vor den anderen wie die Wiesel im Schnee.

So they walked on together, always putting one foot in front of the other like weasels in the snow.

4.1 Zeit genug hatten sie beide,

They both had time enough,

aber wenig zu beißen und zu brechen.   4.2
but little to bite and break.

Wenn sie in eine Stadt kamen, so gingen sie   4.3
umher und grüßten das Handwerk, und, weil das
Schneiderlein so frisch und munter aussah und
so hübsche rote Backen hatte, so gab ihm jeder
gern, und wenn das Glück gut war, so gab ihm die
Meisterstochter unter der Hausthür auch noch einen
Kuß auf den Weg.
When they came to a town, they went about and greeted
the tradesmen, and because the little tailor looked so fresh
and cheerful and had such pretty red cheeks, everyone
liked to give him something, and if his luck was good, the
master's daughter gave him a kiss on the way from under
the house door.

Wenn er mit dem Schuster wieder zusammentraf,   4.4
When he met the cobbler again,

so hatte er immer mehr in seinem Bündel.   4.5
he always had more in his bundle.

Der griesgrämige Schuster schnitt ein schiefes   4.6
Gesicht und meinte,
The grumpy cobbler made a wry face and said,

»Je größer der Schelm, je größer das Glück.«   4.7
"The bigger the rogue, the greater the luck."

Aber der Schneider fing an zu lachen und zu   4.8
singen und teilte alles, was er bekam, mit seinem
Kameraden.
But the tailor began to laugh and sing and shared
everything he got with his companion.

4.9 Klingelten nun ein paar Groschen in seiner Tasche, so ließ er auftragen, schlug vor Freude auf den Tisch, daß die Gläser tanzten, und es hieß bei ihm:

When a few pennies rang in his pocket, he had them served, banged the table with joy so that the glasses danced, and he said:

4.10 »Leicht verdient und leicht verthan.«

"Easily earned and easily done."

5.1 Als sie eine Zeitlang gewandert waren, kamen sie an einen großen Wald, durch welchen der Weg nach der Königsstadt ging.

When they had walked for some time, they came to a large forest through which the road to the royal city ran.

5.2 Es führten aber zwei Fußsteige hindurch, davon war der eine sieben Tage lang, der andere nur zwei Tage, aber niemand von ihnen wußte, welcher der kürzere Weg war.

But there were two footpaths leading through it, one of which was seven days long, the other only two days, but none of them knew which was the shorter way.

5.3 Die zwei Wanderer setzten sich unter einen Eichenbaum und ratschlagten, wie sie sich vorsehen und für wieviel Tage sie Brot mitnehmen wollten.

The two travelers sat down under an oak tree and discussed how they should take care and how many days' worth of bread they should take with them.

5.4 Der Schuster sagte: »Man muß weiter denken als man geht, ich will für sieben Tage Brot mitnehmen.«

The cobbler said, "You have to think further than you walk, I want to take seven days' worth of bread with me."

»Was.« sagte der Schneider, 5.5
"What." said the tailor,

»für sieben Tage Brot auf dem Rücken schleppen wie 5.6
ein Lasttier und sich nicht umschauen?
"carrying bread on your back like a beast of burden for
seven days and not looking back?

Ich halte mich an Gott und kehre mich an nichts. 5.7
I'll stick to God and turn to nothing.

Das Geld, das ich in der Tasche habe, das ist im 5.8
Sommer so gut als im Winter, aber das Brot wird
in der heißen Zeit trocken und obendrein schimmlig.
The money I have in my pocket is as good in summer as in
winter, but the bread gets dry and moldy in the hot season.

Mein Rock geht auch nicht länger als auf die Knöchel. 5.9
My skirt is no longer than my ankles.

Warum sollen wir den richtigen Weg nicht finden? 5.10
Why shouldn't we find the right way?

Für zwei Tage Brot und damit gut.« 5.11
Bread for two days and that's good."

Es kaufte sich also ein jeder sein Brot, 5.12
So they each bought their own bread,

dann gingen sie auf gut Glück in den Wald hinein. 5.13
then went off into the forest at random.

In dem Walde war es so still wie in einer Kirche. 6.1
It was as quiet in the forest as in a church.

6.2 Kein Wind wehte, kein Bach rauschte, kein Vogel sang, und durch die dichtbelaubten Äste drang kein Sonnenstrahl.

No wind blew, no brook rushed, no bird sang, and no ray of sunlight penetrated the dense foliage of the branches.

6.3 Der Schuster sprach kein Wort, ihn drückte das schwere Brot auf dem Rücken, daß ihm der Schweiß über sein verdrießliches und finsteres Gesicht herabfloß.

The shoemaker did not speak a word; the heavy bread on his back weighed him down, so that the sweat poured down his gloomy and morose face.

6.4 Der Schneider aber war ganz munter, sprang daher, pfiff auf einem Blatt oder sang ein Liedchen und dachte:

The tailor, however, was quite lively, jumped about, whistled on a leaf, or sang a little song, and thought,

6.5 »Gott im Himmel muß sich freuen, daß ich so lustig bin.«

"God in heaven must be pleased that I am so merry."

6.6 Zwei Tage ging das so fort, aber als am dritten Tage der Wald kein Ende nehmen wollte und der Schneider sein Brot aufgegessen hatte, so fiel ihm das Herz doch eine Elle tiefer herab;

This went on for two days, but on the third day, when the forest seemed to have no end, and the tailor had eaten his bread, his heart sank a notch;

6.7 indessen verlor er nicht den Mut,

yet he did not lose heart,

6.8 sondern verließ sich auf Gott und auf sein Glück.

but relied on God and his luck.

95

Den dritten Tag legte er sich abends hungrig unter einen Baum und stand den anderen Morgen hungrig wieder auf.

6.9

The third day he lay down hungry under a tree in the evening and got up hungry the next morning.

So ging es auch den vierten Tag, und wenn der Schuster sich auf einen umgestürzten Baum setzte und seine Mahlzeit verzehrte, so blieb dem Schneider nichts als das Zusehen.

6.10

So it went on the fourth day, and when the cobbler sat down on a fallen tree and ate his meal, the tailor had nothing to do but watch.

Bat er um ein Stückchen Brot, so lachte der andere höhnisch und sagte:,

6.11

When he asked for a piece of bread, the other laughed scornfully and said,

»Du bist immer so lustig gewesen, da kannst du auch einmal versuchen wie's thut, wenn man unlustig ist:

6.12

"You have always been so merry, so you might as well try what happens when you are not merry:

die Vögel, die morgens zu früh singen, die stößt abends der Habicht.«

6.13

the birds that sing too early in the morning are killed by the hawk in the evening."

kurz er war ohne Barmherzigkeit.

6.14

He was merciless for a moment.

Aber am fünften Morgen konnte der arme Schneider nicht mehr aufstehen und vor Mattigkeit kaum ein Wort herausbringen;

6.15

But on the fifth morning the poor tailor could not get up, and could scarcely utter a word for weariness;

6.16 die Backen waren ihm weiß und die Augen rot.
his cheeks were white and his eyes red.

6.17 Da sagte der Schuster zu ihm,
Then the cobbler said to him,

6.18 »Ich will dir heute ein Stück Brot geben,
"I will give you a piece of bread today,

6.19 aber dafür will ich dir dein rechtes Auge ausstechen.«
but in return I will gouge out your right eye."

6.20 Der unglückliche Schneider, der doch gern sein
Leben erhalten wollte, konnte sich nicht anders
helfen: er weinte noch einmal mit beiden Augen und
hielt sie dann hin, und der Schuster: der ein Herz von
Stein hatte, stach ihm mit einem scharfen Messer das
rechte Auge aus.
The unhappy tailor, who wanted to keep his life, could not
help himself: he wept once more with both eyes and then
held them out, and the cobbler, who had a heart of stone,
gouged out his right eye with a sharp knife.

6.21 Dem Schneider kam in den Sinn, was ihm sonst seine
Mutter gesagt hatte, wenn er in der Speisekammer
genascht hatte:
The tailor remembered what his mother used to say to him
when he was snacking in the pantry:

6.22 Essen, so viel man mag, und leiden, was man muß.«
"Eat as much as you like, and suffer as much as you must."

Als er sein teuer bezahltes Brot verzehrt hatte, 6.23
machte er sich wieder auf die Beine, vergaß sein
Unglück und tröstete sich damit, daß er mit einem
Auge noch immer genug sehen könnte.
When he had eaten his dearly paid bread, he got back on his
feet, forgot his misfortune and consoled himself with the
fact that he could still see enough with one eye.

Aber am sechsten Tage meldete sich der Hunger aufs 6.24
neue und zehrte ihm fast das Herz auf.
But on the sixth day he was hungry again and his heart was
almost worn out.

Er fiel abends bei einem Baume nieder, und am 6.25
siebenten Morgen konnte er sich vor Mattigkeit
nicht erheben und der Tod saß ihm im Nacken.
In the evening he fell down by a tree, and on the seventh
morning he could not rise for weariness, and death was
breathing down his neck.

Da sagte der Schuster: 6.26
Then the shoemaker said,

»Ich will Barmherzigkeit ausüben und dir nochmals 6.27
Brot geben;
"I will show mercy and give you another loaf of bread;

umsonst bekommst du es nicht, 6.28
you won't get it for nothing,

ich steche dir dafür das andere Auge noch aus.« 6.29
I'll gouge out your other eye for it."

Da erkannte der Schneider sein leichtsinniges Leben, 6.30
Then the tailor recognized his reckless life,

bat den lieben Gott um Verzeihung und sprach: 6.31
asked God for forgiveness and said:

6.32 »Thue, was du mußt, ich will leiden, was ich muß;

"Do what you must, I will suffer what I must;

6.33 aber bedenke, daß unser Herrgott nicht jeden Augenblick richtet und daß eine andere Stunde kommt, wo die böse That vergolten wird, die du an mir verübst und die ich nicht an dir verdient habe.

but remember that our Lord God does not judge every moment and that another hour will come when the evil deed you have done to me will be repaid and which I did not deserve from you.

6.34 Ich habe in guten Tagen mit dir geteilt, was ich hatte.

I have shared with you in good days what I had.

6.35 Mein Handwerk ist derart, daß Stich muß Stich vertreiben.

My craft is such that sting must drive away sting.

6.36 Wenn ich keine Augen mehr habe und nicht mehr nähen kann,

When I have no more eyes and can sew no more,

6.37 so muß ich betteln gehen.

I must go begging.

6.38 Laß mich nur, wenn ich blind bin, hier nicht allein liegen, sonst muß ich verschmachten.«

If I am blind, do not let me lie here alone, or I shall pine away."

6.39 Der Schuster aber, der Gott aus seinem Herzen Vertrieben hatte, nahm das Messer und stach ihm noch das linke Auge aus.

But the cobbler, who had driven God out of his heart, took the knife and gouged out his left eye.

Dann gab er ihm ein Stück Brot zu essen; reichte ihm 6.40
einen Stock und führte ihn hinter sich her.
Then he gave him a piece of bread to eat, handed him a stick
and led him behind him.

Als die Sonne unterging, kamen sie aus dem Walde, 7.1
und vor dem Walde auf dem Felde stand eine Galgen.
When the sun went down, they came out of the forest, and
in front of the forest in the field stood a gallows.

Dahin leitete der Schuster den blinden Schneider, 7.2
There the cobbler led the blind tailor,

ließ ihn dann liegen und ging seiner Wege. 7.3
then left him and went his way.

Vor Müdigkeit, 7.4
The unfortunate man fell asleep from fatigue,

Schmerz und Hunger schlief der Unglückliche ein 7.5
und schlief die ganze Nacht.
pain and hunger and slept all night.

Als der Tag dämmerte, erwachte er, wußte aber nicht 7.6
wo er lag.
When day dawned, he awoke, but did not know where he
lay.

An dem Galgen hingen zwei arme Sünder, 7.7
Two poor sinners were hanging on the gallows,

und auf dem Kopfe eines jeden saß eine Krähe. 7.8
and a crow was sitting on the head of each.

Da fing der eine an zu sprechen: »Bruder, wachst du?« 7.9
Then one of them began to say, "Brother, are you awake?"

7.10   »Ja, ich wache.« antwortete der zweite.

"Yes, I am awake." replied the second.

7.11   »So will ich dir etwas sagen.« fing der erste
wieder an,

"Then I will tell you something." the first began again,

7.12   »der Tau, der heute Nacht über uns vom Galgen
herabgefallen ist, der giebt jedem, der sich damit
wäscht, die Augen wieder.

"the dew that fell on us tonight from the gallows will
restore the eyes of anyone who washes with it.

7.13   Wenn das die Blinden wüßten, wie mancher könnte
sein Gesicht wieder haben, der nicht glaubt, daß das
möglich sei.«

If the blind knew that, how many a man might have his
face restored who does not believe it is possible."

7.14   Als der Schneider das hörte, nahm er sein
Taschentuch, drückte es auf das Gras, und als
es mit dem Tau befeuchtet war, wusch er seine
Augenhöhlen damit.

When the tailor heard this, he took his handkerchief,
pressed it on the grass, and when it was moistened with the
dew, he washed his eye sockets with it.

7.15   Alsbald ging in Erfüllung, was der Gehenkte gesagt
hatte, und ein Paar frische und gesunde Augen
füllten die Höhlen.

Immediately what the hanged man had said came true, and
a pair of fresh and healthy eyes filled the sockets.

7.16   Es dauerte nicht lange, so sah der Schneider die
Sonne hinter den Bergen aufsteigen:

It was not long before the tailor saw the sun rising behind
the mountains:

vor ihm in der Ebene lag die große Königsstadt mit 7.17
ihren prächtigen Thoren und hundert Türmen, und
die goldenen Knöpfe und Kreuze, die auf den Spitzen
standen, fingen an zu glühen.
before him in the plain lay the great royal city with its
magnificent gates and hundred towers, and the golden
buttons and crosses standing on the spires began to glow.

Er unterschied jedes Blatt an den Bäumen, erblickte 7.18
die Vögel, die vorbeiflogen, und die Mücken, die in
der Luft tanzten.
He distinguished every leaf on the trees, saw the birds
flying by and the mosquitoes dancing in the air.

Er holte eine Nähnadel aus der Tasche, und als er den 7.19
Zwirn einfädeln konnte, so gut als er es je gekonnt
hatte, so sprang sein Herz vor Freude.
He took a sewing needle out of his pocket, and when he was
able to thread the thread as well as he had ever been able to,
his heart leapt for joy.

Er warf sich auf seine Knie, dankte Gott für die 7.20
erwiesene Gnade und sprach seinen Morgensegen;
He threw himself on his knees, thanked God for the mercy
he had received, and said his morning blessing;

er vergaß auch nicht für die armen Sünder zu bitten, 7.21
die da hingen wie der Schwengel in der Glocke, und
die der Wind aneinanderschlug.
he did not forget to pray for the poor sinners who were
hanging there like the swinging angel in the bell, and
whom the wind was beating together.

Dann nahm er sein Bündel auf den Rücken, 7.22
Then he took his bundle on his back,

7.23 vergaß bald das ausgestandene Herzeleid und ging unter Singen und Pfeifen weiter.

soon forgot the heartache he had endured and went on his way singing and whistling.

8.1 Das erste, was ihm begegnete, war ein braunes Füllen, das frei im Felde herumsprang.

The first thing he came across was a brown colt, which was running free in the field.

8.2 Er packte es an der Mähne,

He grabbed it by the mane,

8.3 wollte sich aufschwingen und in die Stadt reiten.

wanted to swing himself up and ride into town.

8.4 Das Füllen aber bat um seine Freiheit:

But the colt begged for his freedom:

8.5 »Ich bin noch zu jung.« sprach es,

"I am still too young." he said,

8.6 »auch ein leichter Schneider wie du bricht mir den Rücken entzwei, laß mich laufen, bis ich stark geworden bin.

"even a light tailor like you will break my back, let me run until I am strong.

8.7 Es kommt vielleicht eine Zeit, wo ich dir's lohnen kann.«

Perhaps there will come a time when I can repay you."

8.8 »Lauf hin.« sagte der Schneider,

"Run along." said the tailor,

8.9 »ich sehe, du bist auch so ein Springinsfeld.«

"I see you are also such a jumper."

Er gab ihm noch einen Hieb mit der Gerte über den Rücken, daß es vor Freude mit den Hinterbeinen ausschlug, über Hecken und Gräben setzte und in das Feld hineinjagte.   8.10

He gave him another blow over the back with the whip, so that he kicked out his hind legs with joy, jumped over hedges and ditches and chased into the field.

Aber das Schneiderlein hatte seit gestern nichts gegessen.   9.1

But the little tailor hadn't eaten since yesterday.

»Die Sonne.« sprach er, »füllt mir zwar die Augen,   9.2

"The sun." he said, "fills my eyes,

aber das Brot nicht den Mund.   9.3

but the bread does not fill my mouth.

Das erste, was mir begegnet und halbwegs genießbar ist, das muß herhalten.«   9.4

The first thing I come across that is halfway edible will have to do."

Indem schritt ein Storch ganz ernsthaft über die Wiese daher.   9.5

Then a stork strode earnestly across the meadow.

»Halt, halt.« rief der Schneider und packte ihn am Bein,   9.6

"Stop, stop." cried the tailor, seizing him by the leg,

»ich weiß nicht, ob du zu genießen bist, aber mein Hunger erlaubt mir keine lange Wahl, ich muß dir den Kopf abschneiden und dich braten.«   9.7

"I do not know whether you are fit to eat, but my hunger will not allow me to choose for long; I must cut off your head and roast you."

9.8 »Thue das nicht.« antwortete der Storch,
"Don't do that." replied the stork,

9.9 »ich bin ein heiliger Vogel, dem niemand ein Leid zufügt, und der den Menschen großen Nutzen bringt.
"I am a sacred bird, which no one harms, and which brings great benefit to mankind.

9.10 Läßt du mir mein Leben,
If you let me live,

9.11 so kann ich dir's ein andermal vergelten.«
I can repay you another time."

9.12 »So zieh ab, Vetter Langbein.« sagte der Schneider.
"Off you go, Cousin Longlegs." said the tailor.

9.13 Der Storch erhob sich,
The stork rose up,

9.14 ließ die langen Beine hängen und flog gemächlich fort.
let his long legs hang down and flew away leisurely.

10.1 »Was soll daraus werden?« sagte der Schneider zu sich selbst,
"What is to become of it?" said the tailor to himself,

10.2 »mein Hunger wird immer größer und mein Magen immer leerer.
"my hunger is getting bigger and bigger and my stomach emptier and emptier.

10.3 Was mir jetzt in den Weg kommt, das ist verloren.«
Anything that gets in my way now is lost."

Indem sah er auf einem Teiche ein Paar junge Enten
daherschwimmen. 10.4

Then he saw a pair of young ducks swimming along on a
pond.

»Ihr kommt ja wie gerufen« sagte er, 10.5

"You've come just in time" he said,

packte eine davon und wollte ihr den Hals umdrehen. 10.6

grabbing one of them and trying to wring its neck.

Da fing eine alte Ente, die in dem Schilf steckte, 10.7
laut an zu kreischen, schwamm mit aufgesperrtem
Schnabel herbei und bat ihn flehentlich, sich ihrer
lieben Kinder zu erbarmen.

Then an old duck stuck in the reeds began to screech loudly,
swam over with her beak open and begged him to have
mercy on her dear children.

»Denkst du nicht.« sagte sie, 10.8

"Don't you think." she said,

»wie deine Mutter jammern würde, wenn dich einer 10.9
wegholen und dir den Garaus machen wollte.«

"how your mother would wail if someone wanted to take
you away and finish you off."

»Sei nur still.« sagte der gutmütige Schneider, 10.10

"Be quiet." said the good-natured tailor,

»du sollst deine Kinder behalten.« 10.11

"you shall keep your children."

und setzte die Gefangene wieder ins Wasser. 10.12

and put the prisoner back into the water.

11.1 Als er sich umkehrte, stand er vor einem alten Baum, der halb hohl war, und sah die wilden Bienen aus - und einstiegen.

When he turned back, he stood in front of an old tree that was half hollow and saw the wild bees coming in and out.

11.2 »Da finde ich gleich den Lohn für meine gute That.«

"There I will find the reward for my good deed."

11.3 sagte der Schneider, »der Honig wird mich laben.«

said the tailor, "the honey will refresh me."

11.4 Aber der Weisel kam heraus, drohte und sprach,

But the queen bee came out, threatened and said,

11.5 »Wenn du mein Volk anrührst und mein Nest zerstörst,

"If you touch my colony and destroy my nest,

11.6 so sollen dir unsere Stacheln wie zehntausend glühende Nadeln in die Haut fahren.

our stings shall go into your skin like ten thousand red-hot needles.

11.7 Läßt du uns aber in Ruhe und gehst deiner Wege,

But if you leave us alone and go your way,

11.8 so wollen wir dir ein andermal dafür einen Dienst leisten.«

we will do you a service another time."

12.1 Das Schneiderlein sah, daß auch hier nichts anzufangen war.

The little tailor saw that there was nothing to be done here either.

»Drei Schüsseln leer.« sagte er,

12.2

"Three bowls empty." he said,

»und auf der vierten nichts, das ist eine schlechte
Mahlzeit.«

12.3

"and nothing in the fourth, that's a bad meal."

Er schleppte sich also mit seinem ausgehungerten
Magen in die Stadt, und da es eben zu Mittag läutete,
so war für ihn im Gasthaus schon gekocht und er
konnte sich gleich zu Tisch setzen.

12.4

So he dragged himself into the town with his famished
stomach, and as the bell was just ringing for noon, they had
already cooked for him in the inn, and he was able to sit
down to table at once.

Als er satt war, sagte er:

12.5

When he had eaten his fill, he said:

»Nun will ich auch arbeiten.«

12.6

"Now I want to work too."

Er ging in der Stadt umher, suchte einen Meister und
fand auch bald ein gutes Unterkommen.

12.7

He went around the town looking for a master craftsman
and soon found a good place to stay.

Da er aber sein Handwerk von Grund aus gelernt
hatte, so dauerte es nicht lange, er ward berühmt,
und jeder wollte seinen neuen Rock von dem kleinen
Schneider gemacht haben.

12.8

But as he had learned his trade from scratch, it wasn't long
before he became famous and everyone wanted to have
their new skirt made by the little tailor.

Alle Tage nahm sein Ansehen zu.

12.9

His reputation grew every day.

12.10 »Ich kann in meiner Kunst nicht weiter kommen.« sprach er,

"I can't get any further in my art." he said,

12.11 »und doch geht's jeden Tag besser.«

"and yet it gets better every day."

12.12 Endlich bestellte ihn der König zu seinem Hofschneider.

At last the king appointed him his court tailor.

13.1 Aber wie's in der Welt geht.

But how it goes in the world.

13.2 An demselben Tage war sein ehemaliger Kamerad, der Schuster, auch Hofschuster geworden.

On the same day his former comrade, the cobbler, had also become a court cobbler.

13.3 Als dieser den Schneider erblickte und sah, daß er wieder zwei gesunde Augen hatte, so peinigte ihn das Gewissen.

When he saw the tailor and saw that he had two healthy eyes again, his conscience tormented him.

13.4 »Ehe er Rache an mir nimmt.« dachte er bei sich selbst,

"Before he takes revenge on me." he thought to himself,

13.5 »muß ich ihm eine Grube graben.«

"I must dig him a pit."

13.6 Wer aber anderen eine Grube gräbt, fällt selbst hinein.

But he who digs a pit for others falls into it himself.

Abends, als er Feierabend gemacht hatte und es dämmerig geworden war, schlich er sich zu dem König und sagte:

13.7

In the evening, when he had finished work and it had become dusk, he crept up to the king and said,

»Herr König, der Schneider ist ein übermütiger Mensch und hat sich vermessen, er wollte die goldene Krone wieder herbeischaffen, die vor alten Zeiten ist verloren? gegangen.«

13.8

"Mr. King, the tailor is a high-spirited man and has presumed, he wanted to get back the golden crown that was lost long ago."

»Das sollte mir lieb sein.«

13.9

"I should be glad of that."

sprach der König, ließ den Schneider am anderen Morgen vor sich fordern und befahl ihm, die Krone wieder herbeizuschaffen oder für immer die Stadt zu verlassen.

13.10

said the king, and the next morning he summoned the tailor before him and ordered him to retrieve the crown or leave the city forever.

»Oho.« dachte der Schneider,

13.11

"Oh dear." thought the tailor,

»ein Schelm giebt mehr als er hat.

13.12

"a rogue gives more than he has.

Wenn der murrköpfige König, von mir verlangt, was kein Mensch leisten kann, so will ich nicht warten bis morgen, sondern gleich heute wieder zur Stadt hinaus wandern.«

13.13

If the grumpy king wants me to do what no man can do, I won't wait until tomorrow, but will go out of town today."

110

13.14 Er schnürte also sein Bündel; als er aber aus dem
Thor heraus war, so that es ihm doch leid, daß er sein
Glück ausgehen und die Stadt, in der es ihm so wohl
gegangen war, mit dem Rücken ansehen sollte.

So he tied up his bundle, but when he was out of the gate,
he was sorry that he should spend his fortune and look at
the city, in which he had been so happy, with his back.

13.15 Er kam zu dem Teich, wo er mit den Enten
Bekanntschaft gemacht hatte, da saß gerade die Alte,
der er ihre Jungen gelassen hatte, am Ufer und putzte
sich mit dem Schnabel.

He came to the pond where he had made the acquaintance
of the ducks, and there sat the old woman, to whom he had
left her young, on the bank, preening herself with her beak.

13.16 Sie erkannte ihn gleich und fragte, warum er den
Kopf so hängen lasse.

She recognized him immediately and asked why he was
hanging his head like that.

13.17 »Du wirst dich nicht wundern, wenn du hörst, was
mir begegnet ist.«

"You won't be surprised when you hear what happened to
me."

13.18 antwortete der Schneider und erzählte ihr sein
Schicksal.

the tailor replied and told her his fate.

13.19 »Wenn's weiter nichts ist.« sagte die Ente,

"If it's nothing else." said the duck,

13.20 »da können wir Rat schaffen.

"we can help.

Die Krone ist ins Wasser gefallen und liegt unten auf dem Grunde,

13.21

The crown has fallen into the water and is lying at the bottom,

wie bald haben wir sie wieder heraufgeholt.

13.22

how soon we can get it up again.

Breite nur derweil dein Taschentuch ans Ufer aus.«

13.23

In the meantime, spread out your handkerchief on the shore."

Sie tauchte mit ihren zwölf Jungen unter und nach fünf Minuten war sie wieder oben und saß mitten in der Krone, die auf ihren Fittichen ruhte, und die zwölf Jungen schwammen rund herum, hatten ihre Schnäbel untergelegt und halfen tragen.

13.24

She dived under with her twelve boys and after five minutes she was back on top, sitting in the middle of the crown, which was resting on her wings, and the twelve boys swam all around her, had put their beaks underneath and helped to carry her.

Sie schwammen ans Land und legten die Krone auf das Tuch.

13.25

They swam ashore and placed the crown on the cloth.

»Du glaubst nicht, wie prächtig die Krone war, wenn die Sonne darauf schien, so glänzte sie wie hunderttausend Karfunkelsteine.«

13.26

"You wouldn't believe how splendid the crown was when the sun shone on it, it shone like a hundred thousand carbuncles."

Der Schneider band sein Tuch mit den vier Zipfeln zusammen und trug sie zum König,

13.27

The tailor tied his cloth with the four tails and carried it to the king,

13.28 der in einer Freude war und dem Schneider eine
goldene Kette um den Hals hing.

who was in a state of joy and hung a golden chain around
the tailor's neck.

14.1 Als der Schuster sah, daß der eine Streich mißlungen
war, so besann er sich auf einen zweiten, trat vor den
König und sprach:

When the shoemaker saw that one trick had failed, he
bethought himself of a second, and stood before the King,
and said,

14.2 »Herr König, der Schneider ist wieder so übermütig
geworden, er vermißt sich, das ganze königliche
Schloß, mit allem was darin ist, lose und fest, innen
und außen, in Wachs abzubilden.«

"Sir King, the tailor has again become so overconfident, he
misses the whole royal castle, with all that is in it, loose and
tight, inside and out, in wax."

14.3 Der König ließ den Schneider kommen und befahl
ihm, das ganze königliche Schloß, mit allem was
darin wäre, lose und fest, innen und außen, in Wachs
abzubilden, und wenn er es nicht zustande brächte
oder es fehlte nur ein Nagel an der Wand, so sollte er
zeitlebens unter der Erde gefangen sitzen.

The king sent for the tailor and ordered him to make a
wax copy of the whole royal palace and everything in it,
loose and solid, inside and out, and if he failed to do so, or
if only one nail was missing from the wall, he would be
imprisoned in the ground for the rest of his life.

14.4 Der Schneider dachte: »Es kommt immer Ärger,

The tailor thought, "Trouble always comes,

14.5 das hält kein Mensch aus.«

no man can stand it."

113

warf sein Bündel auf den Rücken und wanderte fort.   14.6
He threw his bundle on his back and wandered off.

Als er an den hohlen Baum kam,   14.7
When he came to the hollow tree,

setzte er sich nieder und ließ den Kopf hängen.   14.8
he sat down and hung his head.

Die Bienen kamen herausgeflogen, und der Weisel   14.9
fragte ihn, ob er einen steifen Hals hätte, weil er den
Kopf so schief hielt.
The bees came flying out and the queen bee asked him if he
had a stiff neck because he was holding his head so crooked.

»Ach nein.« antwortete der Schneider,   14.10
"Oh no." replied the tailor,

»mich drückt etwas anderes.«   14.11
"something else is bothering me."

und er erzählte, was der König von ihm gefordert   14.12
hatte.
and he told them what the king had asked him to do.

Die Bienen fingen an untereinander zu summen und   14.13
zu brummen, und der Weisel sprach:
The bees began to buzz and hum among themselves, and
the queen bee said,

»Geh nur wieder nach Hause, komm aber morgen um   14.14
diese Zeit wieder und bring ein großes Tuch mit, so
wird alles gut gehen.«
"Go home again, but come back tomorrow at this time and
bring a large cloth, and everything will be all right."

14.15 Da kehrte er wieder um, die Bienen aber flogen nach dem königlichen Schloß geradezu in die offenen Fenster hinein, krochen in allen Ecken herum und besahen alles aufs genaueste.

So he turned back, but the bees flew straight into the open windows of the royal palace, crawled around in all the corners and inspected everything very carefully.

14.16 Dann liefen sie zurück und bildeten das Schloß in Wachs nach mit einer solchen Geschwindigkeit, daß man meinte, es wüchse einem vor den Augen.

Then they ran back and reproduced the castle in wax with such speed that one would have thought it was growing before one's eyes.

14.17 Schon am Abend war alles fertig, und als der Schneider am folgenden Morgen kam, so stand das ganze prächtige Gebäude da, und es fehlte kein Nagel an der Wand und kein Ziegel auf dem Dache;

That evening everything was ready, and when the tailor came the next morning, the whole magnificent building was standing there, and not a nail was missing from the wall, nor a tile from the roof;

14.18 dabei war es zart und schneeweiß und roch süß wie Honig.

it was delicate and snow-white, and smelt as sweet as honey.

Der Schneider packte es vorsichtig in sein Tuch und brachte es dem König, der aber konnte sich nicht genug verwundern, stellte es in seinem größten Saal auf und schenkte dem Schneider dafür ein großes steinernes Haus!

14.19

The tailor wrapped it carefully in his cloth and brought it to the king, but he could not be astonished enough, set it up in his greatest hall and gave the tailor a large stone house in return!

Der Schuster aber ließ nicht nach, ging zum drittenmal zu dem König und sprach:

15.1

But the shoemaker did not relent, and went to the king for the third time, and said,

»Herr König, dem Schneider ist zu Ohren gekommen, daß aus dem Schloßhof kein Wasser springen will, da hat er sich vermessen, es solle mitten im Hof mannshoch aufsteigen und hell sein wie Krystall.«

15.2

"Sir King, the tailor has heard that no water will spring out of the palace courtyard, and he has presumed that it should rise as high as a man in the middle of the courtyard and be as bright as crystal."

Da ließ der König den Schneider herbeiholen und sagte:

15.3

Then the king sent for the tailor and said,

»Wenn nicht morgen ein, Strahl von Wasser in meinem Hof springt, wie du versprochen hast, so soll dich der Scharfrichter auf demselben Hof um einen Kopf kürzer machen.«

15.4

"If a stream of water does not spring up in my courtyard tomorrow, as you have promised, the executioner shall cut you off by a head in the same courtyard."

15.5 Der arme Schneider besann sich nicht lange und eilte zum Thor hinaus, und weil es ihm diesmal ans Leben gehen sollte, so rollten ihm die Thränen über die Backen herab.

The poor tailor did not think long and hurried out of the gate, and because this time it was to be his life, the tears rolled down his cheeks.

15.6 Indem er so voll Trauer dahinging, kam das Füllen herangesprungen, dem er einmal die Freiheit geschenkt hatte, und aus dem ein hübscher Brauner geworden war.

As he was walking along thus full of grief, the colt he had once given freedom to, and which had grown into a handsome bay, came jumping up.

15.7 »Jetzt kommt die Stunde.« sprach er zu ihm,

"Now comes the hour." he said to him,

15.8 »wo ich dir deine Gutthat vergelten kann.

"when I can repay you for your good deed.

15.9 Ich weiß schon, was dir fehlt, aber es soll dir bald geholfen werden, sitz nur auf, mein Rücken kann deiner zwei tragen.«

I already know what you lack, but you shall soon be helped, just sit up, my back can carry two of yours."

15.10 Dem Schneider kam das Herz wieder,

The tailor's heart came back to him,

15.11 er sprang in einem Satz auf und das Pferd rannte in vollem Lauf zur Stadt hinein und geradezu auf den Schloßhof.

he jumped up in one leap and the horse ran at full speed into the town and straight into the castle courtyard.

Da jagte es dreimal rund herum, schnell wie der Blitz, und beim drittenmal stürzte es nieder.   15.12

Then it ran three times round and round, as fast as lightning, and the third time it fell down.

In dem Augenblick aber krachte es furchtbar: 15.13

At that moment, however, there was a terrible crash:

ein Stück Erde sprang in der Mitte des Hofes wie eine Kugel in die Lust, und über das Schloß hinaus, und gleich dahinterher erhob sich ein Strahl von Wasser so hoch wie Mann und Pferd, und das Wasser war so rein wie Krystall, und die Sonnenstrahlen fingen an darauf zu tanzen.   15.14

a piece of earth sprang up like a ball in the middle of the courtyard, and out over the castle, and immediately behind it rose a jet of water as high as man and horse, and the water was as pure as crystal, and the sunbeams began to dance on it.

Als der König das sah, stand er vor Verwunderung auf, ging und umarmte das Schneiderlein im Angesicht aller Menschen.   15.15

When the King saw this, he stood up in astonishment, and went and embraced the little tailor in the presence of all the people.

Aber das Glück dauerte nicht lange.   16.1

But their happiness did not last long.

Der König hatte Töchter genug, eine immer schöner als die andere, aber keinen Sohn.   16.2

The king had daughters enough, one always more beautiful than the other, but no son.

16.3 **Da begab sich der boshafte Schuster zum viertenmal zu dem König und sprach:**

Then the mischievous cobbler went to the king for the fourth time and said,

16.4 **»Herr König, der Schneider läßt nicht ab von, seinem Übermut.**

"Sir King, the tailor will not let go of his arrogance.

16.5 **Jetzt hat er sich vermessen. Wenn er wolle,**

Now he has presumed. If he wished,

16.6 **so könne er dem Herrn König einen Sohn durch die Lüfte herbeitragen lassen.«**

he could have a son brought to the king through the air."

16.7 **Der König ließ den Schneider rufen und sprach,**

The king sent for the tailor and said,

16.8 **»Wenn du mir binnen neun Tagen einen Sohn bringen läßt,**

"If you bring me a son within nine days,

16.9 **so sollst du meine älteste Tochter zur Frau haben.«**

you shall have my eldest daughter to wife."

16.10 **»Der Lohn ist freilich groß.« dachte das Schneiderlein,**

"Of course the reward is great." thought the little tailor,

16.11 **»da thäte man wohl ein übriges, aber die Kirschen hängen mir zu hoch: wenn ich danach steige, so bricht unter mir der Ast und ich falle herab.«**

"but the cherries hang too high for me, and if I climb up to them, the branch will break under me and I will fall down."

Er ging nach Hause, setzte sich mit unterschlagenen
Beinen auf seinen Arbeitstisch und bedachte sich,
was zu thun wäre.

16.12

He went home, sat down on his work table with his legs
crossed and thought about what to do.

»Es geht nicht.« rief er endlich aus, »ich will fort,

16.13

"I can't." he finally exclaimed, "I want to leave,

hier kann ich doch nicht in Ruhe leben.«

16.14

I can't live here in peace."

Er schnürte sein Bündel und eilte zum Thore hinaus.

16.15

He tied up his bundle and hurried out of the gate.

Als er auf die Wiesen kam, erblickte er seinen alten
Freund, den Storch, der da, wie ein Weltweiser, auf
- und abging, zuweilen still stand, einen Frosch
in nähere Betrachtung nahm und ihn endlich
verschluckte.

16.16

When he came to the meadows, he saw his old friend, the
stork, pacing up and down like a wise man of the world,
occasionally standing still, taking a closer look at a frog and
finally swallowing it.

Der Storch kam heran und begrüßte ihn. »Ich sehe.«

16.17

The stork approached and greeted him. "I see."

hub er an, »du hast deinen Ranzen auf dem Rücken,

16.18

he began, "you have your satchel on your back,

warum willst du die Stadt verlassen.«

16.19

why do you want to leave the town."

16.20 Der Schneider erzählte ihm, was, der König von ihm verlangt hatte und er nicht erfüllen konnte, und jammerte über sein Mißgeschick.

The tailor told him what the king had asked of him, and what he could not fulfill, and lamented over his misfortune.

16.21 »Laß dir darüber keine grauen Haare wachsen.«

"Don't let your hair grow gray over it."

16.22 sagte der Storch, »ich will dir aus der Not helfen.

said the stork, "I will help you out of your trouble.

16.23 Schon lange bringe ich die Wickelkinder in die Stadt,

I've been taking the babies to town for a long time now,

16.24 da kann ich auch einmal einen kleinen Prinzen aus dem Brunnen holen.

so I can get a little prince out of the well.

16.25 Geh heim und verhalte dich ruhig.

Go home and keep quiet.

16.26 Heute über neun Tage begieb dich in das königliche Schloß,

Go to the royal castle for nine days today,

16.27 da will ich kommen.«

and I will come."

16.28 Das Schneiderlein ging nach Hause und war zu rechter Zeit in dem Schloß.

The little tailor went home and was in the castle at the right time.

16.29 Nicht lange,

Before long,

so kam der Storch herangeflogen und klopfte ans
Fenster.
the stork flew up and knocked at the window.

16.30

Der Schneider öffnete ihm und Vetter Langbein,
stieg vorsichtig herein und ging mit gravitätischen
Schritten über den glatten Marmorboden;
The tailor opened it, and Cousin Longlegs entered carefully,
and walked with grave steps over the smooth marble floor;

16.31

er hatte aber ein Kind im Schnabel,
but he had a child in his beak that was as beautiful as an
angel,

16.32

das schön wie ein Engel war und seine Händchen
nach der Königin ausstreckte.
and stretched out his little hands to the queen.

16.33

Er legte es ihr auf den Schoß,
He laid it on her lap,

16.34

und sie herzte und küßte es und war vor Freude
außer sich.
and she hugged and kissed it and was beside herself with
joy.

16.35

Der Storch nahm, bevor er wieder wegflog, seine
Reisetasche von der Schulter herab und überreichte
sie der Königin.
Before flying away again, the stork took his traveling bag
from his shoulder and handed it to the queen.

16.36

Es steckten Düten darin mit bunten Zuckererbsen,
It contained bags of colorful sweet peas,

16.37

sie wurden unter die kleinen Prinzessinnen verteilt.
which were distributed among the little princesses.

16.38

16.39 **Die älteste aber erhielt nichts, sondern bekam den lustigen Schneider zum Mann.**

The eldest, however, received nothing, but was given the jolly tailor as her husband.

16.40 **»Es ist mir gerade so.«**

"I feel as if I've just won the jackpot."

16.41 **sprach der Schneider, »als Wenn ich das große Los gewonnen hätte.**

said the tailor.

16.42 **Meine Mutter hatte doch recht, die sagte immer:**

My mother was right, she always said:

16.43 **›Wer auf Gott vertraut und nur Glück hat,**

'If you trust in God and only have luck,

16.44 **dem kann's nicht fehlen. «**

you can't go wrong'."

17.1 **Der Schuster mußte die Schuhe machen, in welchen das Schneiderlein auf dem Hochzeitsfest tanzte, hernach ward ihm befohlen, die Stadt auf immer zu verlassen.**

The cobbler had to make the shoes in which the little tailor danced at the wedding feast, after which he was ordered to leave the town forever.

17.2 **Der Weg nach dem Walde führte ihn zu dem Galgen.**

The road to the forest led him to the gallows.

17.3 **Von Zorn, Wut und der Hitze des Tages ermüdet, warf er sich nieder.**

Tired from anger, rage and the heat of the day, he threw himself down.

Als er die Augen zumachte und schlafen wollte,   17.4

As he closed his eyes and wanted to sleep,

stürzten die beiden Krähen von den Köpfen der   17.5
Gehenkten mit lautem Geschrei herab und hackten
ihm die Augen aus.

the two crows swooped down from the heads of the hanged
men with loud cries and pecked out his eyes.

Unsinnig rannte er in den Wald und muß darin   17.6
verschmachtet sein,

He ran madly into the forest and must have languished
there,

denn es hat ihn niemand wieder gesehen oder etwas   17.7
von ihm gehört.

for no one saw or heard from him again.

Rotkäppchen

Little Red Riding Hood

1.1 Es war einmal eine kleine süße Dirne, die hatte jedermann lieb, der sie nur ansah, am allerliebsten aber ihre Großmutter, die wußte gar nicht was sie alles dem Kinde geben sollte.

Once upon a time there was a sweet little maid who loved everyone who looked at her, but most of all her grandmother, who didn't know what to give her child.

1.2 Einmal schenkte sie ihm ein Käppchen von rotem Sammet und weil ihm das so wohl stand, und es nichts anderes mehr tragen wollte, hieß es nur das Rotkäppchen.

Once she gave him a little cap of red velvet, and because it suited him so well, and he would wear nothing else, he was called Little Red Riding Hood.

1.3 Eines Tages sprach seine Mutter zu ihm:

One day his mother said to him:

1.4 »Komm, Rotkäppchen, da hast du ein Stück Kuchen und eine Flasche Wein, bring das der Großmutter hinaus;

"Come, Little Red Riding Hood, you have a piece of cake and a bottle of wine, take it out to his grandmother;

sie ist krank und schwach und wird sich daran laben.   1.5
she is sick and weak and will eat it.

Mach dich auf, bevor es heiß wird, und wenn du   1.6
hinauskommst, so geh hübsch sittsam und lauf nicht
vom Weg ab, sonst fällst du und zerbrichst das Glas
und die Großmutter hat nichts.
Get up before it gets hot, and when you come out, walk
nicely and do not stray from the path, otherwise you
will fall and break the glass and grandmother will have
nothing.

Und wenn du in ihre Stube kommst,   1.7
And when you come into her parlor,

so vergiß nicht guten Morgen zu sagen und guck   1.8
nicht erst in alle Ecken herum.«
don't forget to say good morning and don't look around in
every corner first."

»Ich will schon alles gut machen.«   2.1
"I want to do everything well."

sagte Rotkäppchen zur Mutter, und gab ihr die Hand   2.2
darauf.
said Little Red Riding Hood to her mother and shook her
hand.

Die Großmutter aber wohnte draußen im Wald,   2.3
But her grandmother lived outside in the forest,

eine halbe Stunde vom Dorf.   2.4
half an hour from the village.

2.5 Wie nun Rotkäppchen in den Wald kam, begegnete ihm der Wolf.

As Little Red Riding Hood entered the forest, she met the wolf.

2.6 Rotkäppchen aber wußte nicht was das für ein böses Tier war und fürchtete sich nicht vor ihm.

Little Red Riding Hood did not know what kind of evil animal it was and was not afraid of it.

2.7 »Guten Tag, Rotkäppchen.« sprach er.

"Good day, Little Red Riding Hood." he said.

2.8 »Schönen Dank, Wolf.«

"Thank you very much, wolf."

2.9 »Wohinaus so früh, Rotkäppchen?«

"Where to so early, Little Red Riding Hood?"

2.10 »Zur Großmutter.«

"To my grandmother's."

2.11 »Was trägst du unter der Schürze?«

"What are you wearing under your apron?"

2.12 »Kuchen und Wein, gestern haben wir gebacken, da soll sich die kranke und schwache Großmutter etwas zu gute thun und sich damit stärken.«

"Cake and wine, we baked them yesterday, so that the sick and weak grandmother can treat herself and fortify herself."

2.13 »Rotkäppchen, wo wohnt deine Großmutter?«

"Little Red Riding Hood, where does your grandmother live?"

»Noch eine gute Viertelstunde weiter im Wald, unter den drei großen Eichbäumen, da steht ihr Haus, unten sind die Nußhecken, das wirst du ja wissen.«

2.14

"A good quarter of an hour further on in the forest, under the three big oak trees, that's where her house is, below are the nut hedges, you'll know that."

sagte Rotkäppchen. Der Wolf dachte bei sich:

2.15

said Little Red Riding Hood. The wolf thought to himself,

»Das junge zarte Ding, das ist ein fetter Bissen, der wird noch besser schmecken als die Alte;

2.16

"That tender young thing is a fat morsel, it will taste even better than the old one;

du mußt es listig anfangen, damit du beide erschnappst.«

2.17

you must start cunningly, so that you catch them both."

Da ging er ein Weilchen neben Rotkäppchen her, dann sprach er:

2.18

So he walked along beside Little Red Riding Hood for a little while, then he said,

»Rotkäppchen, sieh einmal die schönen Blumen, die ringsumher stehen, warum guckst du dich nicht um?

2.19

"Little Red Riding Hood, look at the beautiful flowers that are all around you, why don't you look around you?

ich glaube du hörst gar nicht, wie die Vöglein so lieblich singen?

2.20

I don't think you can hear the birds singing so sweetly?

du gehst ja für dich hin als wenn du zur Schule gingst,

2.21

you are walking along as if you were going to school,

2.22 und ist so lustig haußen in dem Wald.«

and it is so funny out in the forest."

3.1 Rotkäppchen schlug die Augen auf, und als es sah wie die Sonnenstrahlen durch die Bäume hin und her tanzten, und alles voll schöner Blumen stand, dachte es,

Little Red Riding Hood opened her eyes, and when she saw how the sun's rays danced to and fro through the trees, and how everything was full of beautiful flowers, she thought,

3.2 »Wenn ich der Großmutter einen frischen Strauß mitbringe,

"If I bring Grandmother a fresh bouquet,

3.3 der wird ihr auch Freude machen:

it will make her happy too:

3.4 es ist so früh am Tage, daß ich doch zu rechter Zeit ankomme.«

it is so early in the day that I shall arrive at the right time."

3.5 lief vom Wege ab in den Wald hinein und suchte Blumen.

She ran off the path into the forest and looked for flowers.

3.6 Und wenn es eine gebrochen hatte, meinte es, weiter hinaus stände eine schönere, und lief danach, und geriet immer tiefer in den Wald hinein.

And when she had broken one, she thought there was a more beautiful one farther on, and ran after it, and got deeper and deeper into the forest.

3.7 Der Wolf aber ging geradeswegs nach dem Hause der Großmutter und klopfte an die Thür.

But the wolf went straight to her grandmother's house and knocked at the door.

»Wer ist draußen?« 3.8
"Who is outside?"

»Rotkäppchen, das bringt Kuchen und Wein, mach 3.9
auf.«
"Little Red Riding Hood, bringing cake and wine, open up."

»Drück nur auf die Klinke.« rief die Großmutter, 3.10
"Just push the door handle." cried the grandmother,

»ich bin zu schwach und kann nicht aufstehen.« 3.11
"I'm too weak and can't get up."

Der Wolf drückte auf die Klinke, die Thür sprang auf 3.12
und er ging, ohne ein Wort zu sprechen, gerade zum
Bett der Großmutter und verschluckte sie.
The wolf pressed the handle, the door burst open, and
without speaking a word he went straight to grandmother's
bed and swallowed her.

Dann that er ihre Kleider an, setzte ihre Haube auf, 3.13
legte sich in ihr Bett und zog die Vorhänge vor.
Then he put on her clothes, put on her hood, lay down in
her bed and drew the curtains.

Rotkäppchen aber war nach den Blumen 4.1
herumgelaufen, und als es so viel zusammen hatte,
daß es keine mehr tragen konnte, fiel ihm die
Großmutter wieder ein und es machte sich auf den
Weg zu ihr.
Little Red Riding Hood, however, had run about after the
flowers, and when she had gathered so many that she could
carry no more, she remembered her grandmother, and
made her way to her.

4.2 **Es wunderte sich, daß die Thür aufstand, und wie es in die Stube trat, so kam es ihm so seltsam darin vor, daß es dachte:**

He was surprised to see the door open, and as he stepped into the parlor it seemed so strange to him that he thought,

4.3 **»Ei, du mein Gott, wie ängstlich wird mir's heute zu Mut, und bin sonst so gern bei der Großmutter!«**

"Oh, my God, how anxious I feel today, and I usually like being with my grandmother so much!"

4.4 **Es rief: »Guten Morgen.« bekam aber keine Antwort.**

He called out, "Good morning." but got no answer.

4.5 **Darauf ging es zum Bett und zog die Vorhänge zurück; da lag die Großmutter, und hatte die Haube tief ins Gesicht gesetzt und sah so wunderlich aus.**

Then she went to the bed and drew back the curtains, and there lay her grandmother, with her hood pulled down over her face, looking so strange.

4.6 **»Ei, Großmutter, was hast du für große Ohren!«**

"Oh, grandmother, what big ears you have!"

4.7 **»Daß ich dich besser hören kann.«**

"So that I can hear you better."

4.8 **»Ei, Großmutter, was hast du für große Augen!«**

"Oh, grandmother, what big eyes you have!"

4.9 **»Daß ich dich besser sehen kann.«**

"So that I can see you better."

4.10 **»Ei, Großmutter, was hast du für große Hände!«**

"Oh, Grandma, what big hands you have!"

»Daß ich dich besser packen kann.« 4.11
"So that I can grab you better."

»Aber, Großmutter, was hast du für ein entsetzlich 4.12
großes Maul!«
"But, Grandma, what a terribly big mouth you have!"

»Daß ich dich besser fressen kann.« 4.13
"So that I can eat you better."

Kaum hatte der Wolf das gesagt, so that er einen Satz 4.14
aus dem Bett und verschlang das arme Rotkäppchen.
No sooner had the wolf said this than he jumped out of bed
and devoured poor Little Red Riding Hood.

Wie der Wolf sein Gelüsten gestillt hatte, legte er sich 5.1
wieder ins Bett, schlief ein und fing an überlaut zu
schnarchen.
When the wolf had satisfied his craving, he went back to
bed, fell asleep and began to snore loudly.

Der Jäger ging eben an dem Hause vorbei und dachte: 5.2
The hunter walked past the house and thought:

»Wie die alte Frau schnarcht, du mußt doch sehen, ob 5.3
ihr etwas fehlt.«
"How the old woman snores, you must see if something is
wrong with her."

Da trat er in die Stube, und wie er vor das Bett kam, 6.1
so sah er, daß der Wolf darin lag.
Then he entered the parlor, and when he came to the bed,
he saw that the wolf was lying in it.

»Finde ich dich hier, du alter Sünder.« sagte er, 6.2
"I'll find you here, you old sinner." he said,

6.3 »ich habe dich lange gesucht.«
"I've been looking for you for a long time."

6.4 Nun wollte er seine Büchse anlegen, da fiel ihm ein, der Wolf könnte die Großmutter gefressen haben, und sie wäre noch zu retten;
Now he was about to put on his rifle, when it occurred to him that the wolf might have eaten his grandmother, and that she could still be saved;

6.5 schoß nicht, sondern nahm eine Schere und fing an dem schlafenden Wolf den Bauch aufzuschneiden.
so he did not shoot, but took a pair of scissors, and began to cut open the sleeping wolf's belly.

6.6 Wie er ein paar Schnitte gethan hatte, da sah er das rote Käppchen leuchten, und noch ein paar Schnitte, da sprang das Mädchen heraus und rief:
When he had made a few cuts, he saw the little red cap glowing, and after a few more cuts, the girl jumped out and cried,

6.7 »Ach, wie war ich erschrocken, wie war's so dunkel in dem Wolf seinem Leib!«
"Oh, how frightened I was, how dark it was in the wolf's belly!"

6.8 Und dann kam die alte Großmutter auch noch lebendig heraus und konnte kaum atmen.
And then the old grandmother came out alive and could hardly breathe.

Rotkäppchen aber holte geschwind große Steine, 6.9
damit füllten sie dem Wolf den Leib, und wie er
aufwachte, wollte er fortspringen, aber die Steine
waren so schwer, daß er gleich niedersank und sich
totfiel.

Little Red Riding Hood, however, quickly fetched large
stones and filled the wolf's body with them, and when he
woke up he wanted to jump away, but the stones were so
heavy that he sank down and fell dead.

Da waren alle drei vergnügt; 7.1

Then all three were happy;

der Jäger zog dem Wolf den Pelz ab und ging damit 7.2
heim, die Großmutter aß den Kuchen und trank den
Wein, den Rotkäppchen gebracht hatte, und erholte
sich wieder, Rotkäppchen aber dachte:

the huntsman took off the wolf's pelt and went home with
it, the grandmother ate the cake and drank the wine that
Little Red Riding Hood had brought, and recovered, but
Little Red Riding Hood thought,

»Du willst dein Lebtag nicht wieder allein vom Wege 7.3
ab in den Wald laufen,

"You don't want to run off the path into the forest alone
again for the rest of your life,

wenn dir's die Mutter verboten hat.« 7.4

if your mother has forbidden it."

8.1 Es wird auch erzählt, daß einmal, als Rotkäppchen der alten Großmutter wieder Gebackenes brachte, ein anderer Wolf ihm zugesprochen und es vom Wege habe ableiten wollen.

It is also said that once, when Little Red Riding Hood was bringing baked goods to her old grandmother, another wolf came to him and wanted to lead him away from the path.

8.2 Rotkäppchen aber hütete sich und ging gerade fort seines Wegs und sagte der Großmutter, daß es dem Wolf begegnet wäre, der ihm guten Tag gewünscht, aber so bös aus den Augen geguckt hätte:

But Little Red Riding Hood was careful and went straight on her way and told her grandmother that she had met the wolf, who had wished her good day, but had looked so evil out of his eyes:

8.3 »Wenn's nicht auf offener Straße gewesen wäre,

"If it hadn't been on the open road,

8.4 er hätte mich gefressen.«

he would have eaten me."

8.5 »Komm.« sagte die Großmutter,

"Come." said the grandmother,

8.6 »wir wollen die Thür verschließen, daß er nicht herein kann.«

"let's lock the door so he can't get in."

8.7 Bald danach klopfte der Wolf an und rief:

Soon afterward the wolf knocked and cried,

8.8 »Mach auf, Großmutter, ich bin das Rotkäppchen, ich bring dir Gebackenes.«

"Open up, grandmother, I am Little Red Riding Hood, and I will bring you something to eat."

Sie schwiegen aber still und machten die Thür nicht auf; 8.9

But they were silent and did not open the door;

da schlich der Graukopf etliche Male um das Haus, sprang endlich aufs Dach und wollte warten bis Rotkäppchen abends nach Haus ginge, dann wollte er ihm nachschleichen und wollt's in der Dunkelheit fressen. 8.10

then the gray wolf crept around the house several times, finally jumped up on the roof and wanted to wait until Little Red Riding Hood went home in the evening, then he wanted to sneak after her and eat her in the dark.

Aber die Großmutter merkte, was er im Sinn hatte. 8.11

But the grandmother realized what he had in mind.

Nun stand vor dem Hause ein großer Steintrog, 8.12

Now there was a large stone trough in front of the house,

da sprach sie zu dem Kinde: 8.13

and she said to the child:

»Nimm den Eimer, Rotkäppchen, gestern habe ich Würste gekocht, da trag das Wasser, worin sie gekocht sind, in den Trog.« 8.14

"Take the bucket, Little Red Riding Hood, yesterday I cooked sausages, so carry the water in which they are cooked into the trough."

Rotkäppchen trug so lange, bis der große, große Trog ganz voll war. 8.15

Little Red Riding Hood carried on until the big, big trough was completely full.

8.16 Da stieg der Geruch von den Würsten dem Wolf in die Nase, er schnupperte und guckte hinab, endlich machte er den Hals so lang, daß er sich nicht mehr halten konnte und anfing zu rutschen;

Then the smell of the sausages got into the wolf's nose, he sniffed and looked down, and at last he stretched his neck so long that he could no longer hold on and began to slide;

8.17 so rutschte er vom Dach herab,

so he slipped down from the roof,

8.18 gerade in den großen Trog hinein und ertrank.

straight into the big trough and drowned.

8.19 Rotkäppchen aber ging fröhlich nach Haus, und that ihm niemand etwas zuleide.

Little Red Riding Hood, however, went merrily home, and did him no harm.

Hans mein Igel

Hans my Hedgehog

1.1 Es war einmal ein Bauer, der hatte Geld und Gut genug, aber wie reich er war, so fehlte doch etwas an seinem Glück:

Once upon a time there was a farmer who had enough money and goods, but however rich he was, there was something missing from his happiness:

1.2 er hatte mit seiner Frau keine Kinder.

he and his wife had no children.

1.3 Öfters, wenn er mit den anderen Bauern in die Stadt ging, spotteten sie und fragten, warum er keine Kinder hätte.

Often, when he went into town with the other farmers, they mocked him and asked why he had no children.

1.4 Da ward er endlich zornig, und als er nach Hause kam, sprach er:

He finally got angry and when he came home, he said:

1.5 »Ich will ein Kind haben, und sollt's ein Igel sein.«

"I want to have a child, and it should be a hedgehog."

Da kriegte seine Frau ein Kind, das war oben ein
Igel und unten ein Junge, und als sie das Kind sah,
erschrak sie und sprach,

1.6

Then his wife had a child, which was a hedgehog on the top
and a boy on the bottom, and when she saw the child, she
was frightened and said,

»Siehst du, du hast uns verwünscht.« Da sprach der
Mann:

1.7

"You see, you have cursed us." Then the man said,

»Was kann das alles helfen, getauft muß der Junge
werden, aber wir können keinen Gevatter dazu
nehmen.«

1.8

"What good can all this do, the boy must be baptized, but
we cannot take a godfather for him."

Die Frau sprach:

1.9

The woman said,

»Wir können ihn auch nicht anders taufen als Hans
mein Igel.«

1.10

"We cannot baptize him otherwise than as Hans my
hedgehog."

Als er getauft war, sagte der Pfarrer:

1.11

When he was baptized, the priest said,

»Der kann wegen seiner Stacheln in kein ordentlich
Bett kommen.«

1.12

"He can't get into a proper bed because of his spines."

Da ward hinter dem Ofen ein wenig Stroh
zurechtgemacht und Hans mein Igel darauf gelegt.

1.13

So a little straw was made up behind the stove and Hans my
hedgehog was laid on it.

1.14 Er konnte auch an der Mutter nicht trinken,
He couldn't drink from his mother either,

1.15 denn er hätte sie mit seinen Stacheln gestochen.
because he would have pricked her with his thorns.

1.16 So lag er da hinter dem Ofen acht Jahre und sein
Vater war ihn müde und dachte, wenn er nur stürbe;
So he lay there behind the stove for eight years, and his
father was tired of him, and thought if he would only die;

1.17 aber er starb nicht, sondern blieb da liegen.
but he did not die, but remained there.

1.18 Nun trug es sich zu, daß in der Stadt ein Markt war,
und der Bauer wollte hingehen, da fragte er seine
Frau, was er ihr sollte mitbringen.
Now it happened that there was a market in the town,
and the farmer wanted to go, so he asked his wife what he
should bring her.

1.19 »Ein wenig Fleisch und ein paar Wecke,
"A little meat and a few buns,

1.20 was zum Haushalt gehört.« sprach sie.
what belongs to the household." she said.

1.21 Darauf fragte er die Magd,
Then he asked the maid,

1.22 die wollte ein paar Toffeln und Zwickelstrümpfe.
who wanted some potatoes and stockings.

1.23 Endlich sagte er auch: »Hans mein Igel,
At last he said, "Hans my hedgehog,

was willst du denn haben?« 1.24

what do you want?"

»Väterchen.« sprach er, 1.25

"Father." he said,

»bring mir doch einen Dudelsack mit.« 1.26

"bring me a bagpipe."

Wie nun der Bauer wieder nach Hause kam, gab 1.27
er der Frau, was er ihr gekauft hatte, Fleisch und
Wecke, dann gab er der Magd die Toffeln und die
Zwickelstrümpfe, endlich ging er hinter den Ofen
und gab dem Hans mein Igel den Dudelsack.

When the farmer came home again, he gave his wife what
he had bought her, meat and buns, then he gave the maid
the potatoes and the stockings, and finally he went behind
the stove and gave Hans my hedgehog the bagpipes.

Und wie Hans mein Igel den Dudelsack hatte, 1.28
sprach er:

And when Hans my hedgehog had the bagpipes, he said,

»Väterchen, geht doch vor die Schmiede und laßt 1.29
mir meinen Göckelhahn beschlagen, dann will ich
fortreiten und will nimmermehr wiederkommen.«

"Father, go to the smithy and have my cock shod, then I will
ride away and never come back."

Da war der Bauer froh, daß er ihn los werden sollte, 1.30
und ließ ihm den Hahn beschlagen, und als er fertig
war, setzte sich Hans mein Igel darauf, ritt fort,
nahm auch Schweine und Esel mit, die wollte er
draußen im Walde hüten.

Then the farmer was glad to be rid of him, and had the cock
shod for him, and when it was done, Hans my hedgehog
sat on it, rode away, and took pigs and donkeys with him,
which he wanted to herd out in the forest.

1.31 Im Walde aber mußte der Hahn mit ihm auf einen hohen Baum fliegen, da saß er und hütete die Esel und Schweine, und saß lange Jahre, bis die Herde ganz groß war, und wußte sein Vater nichts von ihm.

But in the forest the cock had to fly with him up a high tree, and there he sat and herded the donkeys and pigs, and sat for many years, until the herd was quite large, and his father knew nothing of him.

1.32 Wenn er aber auf dem Baume saß, blies er seinen Dudelsack und machte Musik, die war sehr schön.

But when he sat in the tree, he played his bagpipes and made music, which was very beautiful.

1.33 Einmal kam ein König vorbeigefahren,

Once a king came by,

1.34 der hatte sich verirrt und hörte die Musik:

who had lost his way and heard the music:

1.35 da verwunderte er sich darüber und schickte seinen Bedienten hin, er sollte sich einmal umgucken, wo die Musik herkäme.

he was astonished at it and sent his servant to look around to see where the music was coming from.

1.36 Er guckte sich um, sah aber nichts als ein kleines Tier auf dem Baume oben sitzen, das war wie ein Göckelhahn, auf dem ein Igel saß, und der machte die Musik.

He looked around, but saw nothing but a small animal sitting on the tree above, which was like a cockerel with a hedgehog sitting on it, and it was making the music.

143

Da sprach der König zum Bedienten, er sollte fragen, warum er da säße, und ob er nicht wüßte, wo der Weg in sein Königreich ginge.

1.37

Then the king said to the servant that he should ask him why he was sitting there, and whether he did not know the way to his kingdom.

Da stieg Hans mein Igel vom Baum und sprach, er wollte den Weg zeigen, wenn der König ihm wollte verschreiben und versprechen, was ihm zuerst begegnete am königlichen Hofe, sobald er nach Hause käme.

1.38

Then Hans my hedgehog got down from the tree and said he would show the way if the king would prescribe and promise him what he would first meet at the royal court as soon as he came home.

Da dachte der König:

1.39

Then the king thought,

»Das kann ich leicht thun, Hans mein Igel versteht's doch nicht, und ich kann schreiben, was ich will.«

1.40

"I can easily do that, Hans my hedgehog does not understand, and I can write what I like."

Da nahm der König Feder und Tinte und schrieb etwas auf, und als es geschehen war, zeigte ihm Hans mein Igel den Weg, und er kam glücklich nach Hause.

1.41

So the King took pen and ink and wrote something down, and when it was done, Hans my Hedgehog showed him the way, and he came home happily.

Seine Tochter aber, wie sie ihn von weitem sah, war so voll Freude, daß sie ihm entgegenlief und ihn küßte.

1.42

But his daughter, when she saw him from afar, was so full of joy that she ran to meet him and kissed him.

1.43 Da gedachte er an Hans mein Igel, und erzählte ihr, wie es ihm gegangen wäre, und daß er einem wunderlichen Tier hätte verschreiben sollen, was ihm daheim zuerst begegnen würde, und das Tier hätte auf einem Hahn wie aus einem Pferde gesessen und schöne Musik gemacht;

Then he thought of Hans my Hedgehog, and told her how he had fared, and that he had been told to write to a strange animal what he would first meet with at home, and that the animal had sat on a cock like a horse, and made beautiful music;

1.44 er hätte aber geschrieben, es sollt's nicht haben, denn Hans mein Igel könnte es doch nicht lesen.

but he had written that it should not have it, for Hans my Hedgehog could not read it.

1.45 Darüber war die Prinzessin froh und sagte, das wäre gut, denn sie wäre doch, nimmermehr hingegangen.

The princess was glad of this, and said it would be well, for she would never have gone.

2.1 Hans mein Igel aber hütete die Esel und Schweine, war immer lustig, saß auf dem Baume und blies auf seinem Dudelsack.

Hans my hedgehog, however, tended the donkeys and pigs, was always merry, sat in the tree and played his bagpipes.

2.2 Nun geschah es, daß ein anderer König gefahren kam mit seinen Bedienten und Läufern und hatte sich verirrt und wußte nicht wieder nach Hause zu kommen, weil der Wald so groß war.

Now it happened that another king came with his servants and runners and had lost his way and did not know how to get home again because the forest was so large.

Da hörte er gleichfalls die schöne Musik von weitem und sprach zu seinem Läufer, was das wohl wäre, er sollte einmal zusehen.   2.3

Then he also heard the beautiful music from afar, and said to his runner what it was, he should go and see it.

Da ging der Läufer hin unter den Baum und sah den Göckelhahn sitzen und Hans mein Igel obendrauf.   2.4

So the runner went under the tree and saw the cockerel sitting there and Hans my hedgehog on top.

Der Läufer fragte ihn, was er da oben vorhätte.   2.5

The runner asked him what he was doing up there.

»Ich hüte meine Esel und Schweine; aber was ist Euer Begehren?«   2.6

"I'm looking after my donkeys and pigs, but what do you want?"

Der Läufer sagte, sie hätten sich verirrt und könnten nicht wieder ins Königreich, ob er ihnen den Weg nicht zeigen wollte.   2.7

The runner said that they had lost their way and could not get back to the kingdom, if he did not want to show them the way.

Da stieg Hans mein Igel mit dem Hahn vom Baume herunter und sagte zu dem alten König, er wolle ihm den Weg zeigen, wenn er ihm zu eigen geben wollte, was ihm zu Hause vor seinem königlichen Schlosse das erste begegnen würde.   2.8

Then Hans my hedgehog came down from the tree with the cock, and said to the old king that he would show him the way if he would give him what he would first meet with at home in front of his royal castle.

Der König sagte »ja«   2.9

The king said "yes"

2.10 und unterschrieb sich dem Hans mein Igel, er sollte es haben.

and signed to Hans my Hedgehog that he should have it.

2.11 Als das geschehen war, ritt er auf dem Göckelhahn voraus und zeigte ihm den Weg, und gelangte der König glücklich wieder in sein Reich.

When this was done, he rode ahead on the goat-cock and showed him the way, and the king returned happily to his kingdom.

2.12 Wie er auf den Hof kam, war große Freude darüber.

When he arrived at the court, there was great joy.

2.13 Nun hatte er eine einzige Tochter, die war sehr schön, die lief ihm entgegen, fiel, ihm um den Hals und küßte ihn und freute sich, daß ihr alter Vater wieder kam.

Now he had an only daughter, who was very beautiful, and she ran to meet him, fell on his neck and kissed him, and was glad that her old father had come back.

Sie fragte ihn auch, wo er so lange in der Welt 2.14
gewesen wäre, da erzählte er ihr, er hätte sich verirrt
und wäre beinahe gar nicht wiedergekommen, aber
als er durch einen großen Wald gefahren wäre,
hätte einer, halb wie ein Igel, halb wie ein Mensch,
rittlings auf einem Hahn in einem hohen Baum
gesessen und schöne Musik gemacht, der hätte ihm
fortgeholfen und den Weg gezeigt, er aber hätte ihm
dafür versprochen, was ihm am königlichen Hofe
zuerst begegnete, und das wäre sie, und das thäte
ihm nun so leid.

She also asked him where he had been so long in the world,
and he told her that he had lost his way, and had almost
never come back, but that when he had passed through a
great forest, some one, half like a hedgehog, half like a man,
had sat astride a cock in a high tree, and made beautiful
music, who had helped him away and shown him the way,
but he had promised him in return what he had first met at
the royal court, and that was her, and he was now so sorry
for that.

Da versprach sie ihm, sie wollte gern mit ihm gehen 2.15
wenn er käme, ihrem alten Vater zuliebe.

So she promised him that she would gladly go with him
when he came, for her old father's sake.

Hans mein Igel aber hütete seine Schweine, und die 3.1
Schweine bekamen wieder Schweine, und wurden
ihrer so viel, daß der ganze Wald voll war.

But Hans my hedgehog tended his pigs, and the pigs got
pigs again, and became so many that the whole forest was
full.

3.2 Da wollte Hans mein Igel nicht länger im Walde leben, und ließ seinem Vater sagen, sie sollten alle Ställe im Dorfe räumen, denn er käme mit einer so großen Herde, daß jeder schlachten könnte, der nur schlachten wollte.

Then Hans my Hedgehog no longer wanted to live in the forest, and told his father that they should clear out all the stables in the village, for he was coming with such a large herd that anyone who wanted to slaughter could do so.

3.3 Da war sein Vater betrübt, als er das hörte, denn er dachte, Hans mein Igel wäre schon lange gestorben.

His father was saddened when he heard this, for he thought that Hans my Hedgehog had died long ago.

3.4 Hans mein Igel aber setzte sich auf seinen Göckelhahn, trieb die Schweine vor sich her ins Dorf und ließ schlachten;

Hans my hedgehog, however, sat on his goat's cock, drove the pigs before him into the village and had them slaughtered;

3.5 hu!

hu!

3.6 da war ein Gemetzel und ein Hacken, daß man's zwei Stunden weit hören konnte.

there was a slaughter and a hacking that could be heard for two hours.

3.7 Danach sagte Hans mein Igel:

Afterwards Hans my hedgehog said,

»Väterchen, laßt mir meinen Göckelhahn noch   3.8
einmal vor der Schmiede beschlagen, dann reite,
ich fort und komme mein Lebtag nicht wieder.«
"Father, let me have my cockerel shod once more in front of
the smithy, then I'll ride away and never come back for the
rest of my life."

Da ließ der Vater den Göckelhahn beschlagen und   3.9
war froh, daß Hans mein Igel nicht wieder kommen
wollte.
So the father had the cockerel shod and was glad that Hans
my hedgehog did not want to come back.

Hans mein Igel ritt fort in das erste Königreich, da   4.1
hatte der König befohlen, wenn einer käme auf
einem Hahn geritten und hätte einen Dudelsack
bei sich, dann sollten alle auf ihn schießen, hauen
und stechen, damit er nicht ins Schloß käme.
Hans my Hedgehog rode away into the first kingdom,
where the King had given orders that if any one came riding
on a cock and had a bagpipe with him, they were all to
shoot, beat, and stab him, so that he should not get into the
castle.

Als nun Hans mein Igel dahergeritten kam, drangen   4.2
sie mit den Bajonetten auf ihn ein, aber er gab dem
Hahn die Sporen, flog auf, über das Thor hin vor des
Königs Fenster, ließ sich da nieder und rief ihm zu,
er sollt' ihm geben, was er versprochen hätte, sonst
wollte er ihm und seiner Tochter das Leben nehmen.
When Hans my Hedgehog came riding along, they came at
him with their bayonets, but he gave the spurs to the cock,
flew up, over the gate to the king's window, sat down there
and called out to him that he should give him what he had
promised, otherwise he would take his life and that of his
daughter.

4.3 Da gab der König seiner Tochter gute Worte, sie möchte zu ihm hinausgehen, damit sie ihm und sich das Leben rettete.

Then the king gave his daughter good words to go out to him, that she might save his life and her own.

4.4 Da zog sie sich weiß an, und ihr Vater gab ihr einen Wagen mit sechs Pferden und herrliche Bedienten, Geld und Gut.

So she dressed herself in white, and her father gave her a carriage with six horses and splendid attendants, money and goods.

4.5 Sie setzte sich ein, und Hans mein Igel mit seinem Hahn und Dudelsack neben sie, dann nahmen sie Abschied und zogen fort, und der König dachte, er kriegte sie nicht wieder zu sehen.

She sat down, and Hans my hedgehog with his cock and bagpipes beside her, then they took their leave and departed, and the King thought he would never see her again.

4.6 Es ging aber anders als er dachte, denn als sie ein Stück Wegs von der Stadt waren, da zog ihr Hans mein Igel die schönen Kleider aus und stach sie mit seiner Igelhaut, bis sie ganz blutig war, und sagte:

But it did not turn out as he thought, for when they were a little way from the town, Hans my Hedgehog took off her beautiful clothes, and pricked her with his hedgehog's skin till she was all bloody, and said,

4.7 »Das ist der Lohn für eure Falschheit, geh hin, ich will dich nicht.«

"This is the reward for your falsehood, go away, I don't want you."

4.8 und jagte sie damit nach Hause,

and chased her home with it,

und war sie beschimpft ihr Lebtag.   4.9

and she was insulted all her life.

Hans mein Igel aber ritt weiter auf seinem   5.1
Göckelhahn und mit seinem Dudelsack nach dem
zweiten Königreich, wo er dem König auch den Weg
gezeigt hatte.

Hans my hedgehog, however, rode on to the second
kingdom on his cockerel and with his bagpipes, where
he had also shown the king the way.

Der aber hatte bestellt, wenn einer käme, wie Hans   5.2
mein Igel, sollten sie das Gewehr präsentieren, ihn
frei hereinführen, Vivat rufen und ihn ins Schloß
bringen.

But the king had ordered that if someone like Hans my
Hedgehog came, they should present the gun, lead him in
freely, shout vivat and bring him into the castle.

Wie ihn nun die Königstochter sah, war sie   5.3
erschrocken, weil er doch gar zu wunderlich aussah,
sie dachte aber, es wäre nicht anders, sie hätte es
ihrem Vater versprochen.

When the king's daughter saw him, she was frightened
because he looked too strange, but she thought it could not
be otherwise, she had promised her father.

Da ward Hans mein Igel von ihr bewillkommnet,   5.4
und ward mit ihr vermählt, und er mußte mit an die
königliche Tafel gehen, und sie setzte sich an seine
Seite, und sie aßen und tranken.

Then Hans my hedgehog was welcomed by her, and was
married to her, and he had to go with her to the royal table,
and she sat down by his side, and they ate and drank.

5.5 Wie's nun Abend ward, daß sie wollten schlafen gehen, da fürchtete sie sich sehr vor seinen Stacheln;

When evening came, and they were about to go to bed, she was very much afraid of his thorns;

5.6 er aber sprach, sie sollte sich nicht fürchten, es geschähe ihr kein Leid, und sagte zu dem alten König, er sollte vier Mann bestellen, die sollten wachen vor der Kammerthür und ein großes Feuer anmachen, und wenn er in die Kammer eingehe und sich ins Bett legen wollte, würde er aus seiner Igelhaut herauskriechen und sie vor dem Bett liegen lassen;

but he said she should not be afraid, she would not be harmed, and told the old King that he should order four men to keep watch at the door of the chamber, and light a great fire, and when he entered the chamber and went to bed, he would crawl out of his hedgehog's skin and leave her lying in front of the bed;

5.7 dann sollten die Männer hurtig herbeispringen und sie ins Feuer werfen, auch dabei bleiben, bis sie vom Feuer verzehrt wäre.

Then the men were to rush up and throw it into the fire, and stay there until it was consumed by the fire.

5.8 Wie die Glocke nun elf schlug, da ging er in die Kammer, streifte die Igelhaut ab und ließ sie vor dem Bett liegen: da kamen die Männer und holten sie geschwind und warfen sie ins Feuer; und als sie das Feuer verzehrt hatte, da war er erlöst und lag da im Bett ganz als ein Mensch gestaltet, aber er war kohlschwarz wie gebrannt.

When the bell struck eleven, he went into the chamber, stripped off the hedgehog's skin, and left it lying in front of the bed; then the men came and fetched it quickly, and threw it into the fire; and when the fire had consumed it, he was delivered, and lay there in bed quite fashioned like a man, but he was coal-black as if he had been burnt.

Der König schickte zu seinem Arzt, der wusch ihn mit   5.9
guten Salben und balsamierte ihn, da ward er weiß,
und war ein schöner junger Herr.
The king sent to his physician, who washed him with good
ointments and embalmed him, and he became white, and
was a handsome young gentleman.

Wie das die Königstochter sah, war sie froh, und am   5.10
anderen Morgen standen sie mit Freuden auf, aßen
und tranken, und ward die Vermählung erst recht
gefeiert, und Hans mein Igel bekam das Königreich
von dem alten König.
When the King's daughter saw this, she was glad, and the
next morning they arose with joy, ate and drank, and the
marriage was more than ever celebrated, and Hans my
hedgehog received the kingdom from the old King.

Wie etliche Jahre herum waren, fuhr er mit seiner   6.1
Gemahlin zu seinem Vater und sagte, er wäre sein
Sohn.
When several years had passed, he and his wife went to his
father and said that he was his son.

Der Vater aber sprach, er hatte keinen, er hätte nur   6.2
einen gehabt, der wäre aber wie ein Igel mit Stacheln
geboren worden und wäre in die Welt gegangen.
But the father said that he had none, that he had only had
one, but that he had been born like a hedgehog with thorns
and had gone into the world.

Da gab er sich zu erkennen,   6.3
So he made himself known,

und der alte Vater freute sich und ging mit ihm in   6.4
sein Königreich.
and the old father rejoiced and went with him to his
kingdom.

Mein Märchen ist aus,

und geht vor Gustchen sein Haus.

My fairy tale is over,

and goes outside Gustchen's house.

Das Totenhemdchen

The Shroud

1.1 Es hatte eine Mutter eine Büblein von sieben Jahren, das war so schön und lieblich, daß es niemand ansehen konnte, ohne ihm gut zu sein, und sie hatte es auch lieber als alles auf der Welt.

There was a mother who had a little girl seven years old, who was so beautiful and lovely that no one could look at her without being kind to her, and she loved her better than anything in the world.

1.2 Nun geschah es,

Now it happened that she suddenly fell ill,

1.3 daß es plötzlich krank ward und der liebe Gott es zu sich nahm;

and the good God took her to Himself;

1.4 darüber könnte sich die Mutter nicht trösten und weinte Tag und Nacht.

and her mother could not comfort herself about it, and wept day and night.

Bald darauf aber, nachdem es begraben war, zeigte
sich das Kind nachts an den Plätzen, wo es sonst im
Leben gesessen und gespielt hatte;

1.5

Soon afterwards, however, after it had been buried, the
child showed itself at night in the places where it had
usually sat and played in life;

weinte die Mutter, so weinte es auch, und wenn der
Morgen kam, war es verschwunden.

1.6

if the mother wept, it wept also, and when morning came it
had disappeared.

Als aber die Mutter gar nicht aufhören wollte zu
weinen, kam es in einer Nacht mit seinem weißen
Totenhemdchen, in welchem es in den Sarg gelegt
war, und mit dem Kränzchen aus dem Kopf, setzte
sich zu ihren Füßen auf das Bett, und sprach:

1.7

But when her mother would not stop crying, she came one
night with her white shroud, in which she had been laid
in the coffin, and with the wreath from her head, and sat
down on the bed at her feet, and said,

»Ach, Mutter, höre doch auf zu weinen, sonst kann
ich in meinem Sarge nicht einschlafen, denn mein
Totenhemdchen wird nicht trocken von deinen
Thränen, die alle darauf fallen.«

1.8

"Oh, mother, do stop crying, or I shall not be able to sleep
in my coffin, for my shroud will not dry from your tears,
which all fall on it."

Da erschrak die Mutter, als sie das hörte und weinte
nicht mehr.

1.9

The mother was frightened when she heard this and
stopped crying.

1.10 Und in der anderen Nacht kam das Kindchen wieder, hielt in der Hand ein Lichtchen und sagte:

And the next night the child came again, holding a little light in her hand, and said,

1.11 »Siehst du, nun ist mein Hemdchen bald trocken und ich habe Ruhe in meinem Grabe.«

"You see, now my shroud will soon be dry, and I shall have peace in my grave."

1.12 Da befahl die Mutter dem lieben Gott ihr Leid und ertrug es still und geduldig, und das Kind kam nicht wieder, sondern schlief in seinem unterirdischen Bettchen.

So the mother gave her sorrow to God and bore it quietly and patiently, and the child did not come back, but slept in its underground bed.

Der Jude im Dorn

The Jew in the Thorn

1.1 Es war einmal ein reicher Mann, der hatte einen Knecht, der diente ihm fleißig und redlich, war alle Morgen der erste aus dem Bett und abends der letzte hinein, und wenn's eine saure Arbeit gab, wo keiner anpacken wollte, so stellte er sich immer zuerst daran.

Once upon a time there was a rich man who had a servant who served him diligently and honestly, was the first out of bed every morning and the last in at night, and if there was sour work that no one wanted to do, he always got to it first.

1.2 Dabei klagte er nicht,

He never complained,

1.3 sondern war mit allem zufrieden und war immer lustig.

but was happy with everything and was always cheerful.

1.4 Als sein Jahr herum war,

When his year was up,

1.5 gab ihm der Herr keinen Lohn und dachte:

the master didn't give him any wages and thought:

161

»Das ist das gescheitste, so spare ich etwas und
er geht mir nicht weg, sondern bleibt hübsch im
Dienst.«

1.6

"That's the smartest thing to do, so I'll save a bit and he
won't leave me, but will stay in service."

Der Knecht schwieg auch still, that das zweite
Jahr wie das erste seine Arbeit, und als er am Ende
desselben abermals keinen Lohn bekam, ließ er sich's
gefallen und blieb noch länger.

1.7

The servant also kept quiet, did his work for the second year
as well as the first, and when he again received no wages
at the end of that year, he put up with it and stayed even
longer.

Als auch das dritte Jahr herum war, bedachte sich der
Herr, griff in die Tasche, holte aber nichts heraus.

1.8

When the third year was over, the master thought about it,
reached into his pocket, but took nothing out.

Da fing der Knecht endlich an und sprach:

1.9

Then the servant finally started and said:

»Herr, ich habe drei Jahre redlich gedient, seid so gut
und gebt mir, was mir von Rechts wegen zukommt;

1.10

"Sir, I have served you honestly for three years, be so good
as to give me what is due to me by right;

ich will fort und mich gern weiter in der Welt
umsehen.«

1.11

I want to go away and look around the world again."

Da antwortete der Geizhals:

1.12

The miser replied:

1.13 »Ja, mein Knecht, du hast mir unverdrossen gedient, dafür sollst du mildiglich belohnt werden.«

"Yes, my servant, you have served me unflaggingly, and you shall be mildly rewarded for it."

1.14 griff abermals in die Tasche und zählte dem Knecht drei Heller einzeln auf.

He reached into his pocket again and counted out three pennies one by one for the servant.

1.15 »Da hast du für jedes Jahr einen Heller, das ist ein großer und reichlicher Lohn, wie du ihn bei wenigen Herren empfangen hättest.«

"There you have a farthing for every year, that is a great and ample reward, such as you would have received from few masters."

1.16 Der gute Knecht, der vom Geld wenig verstand, strich sein Kapital ein und dachte:

The good servant, who knew little about money, pocketed his capital and thought:

1.17 »Nun hast du vollauf in der Tasche,

"Now you have plenty in your pocket,

1.18 was willst du sorgen und dich mit schwerer Arbeit länger plagen.«

what do you want to worry about and toil longer with hard work."

2.1 Da zog er fort, bergauf, bergab, sang und sprang nach Herzenslust.

So he went off, uphill, downhill, singing and jumping to his heart's content.

Nun trug es sich zu, als er an einem Buschwerk vorüberkam, daß ein kleines Männchen hervortrat und ihn anrief:

2.2

Now it happened, as he passed a bush, that a little man stepped out and called to him:

»Wo hinaus, Bruder Lustig?

2.3

"Where are you going, Brother Lustig?

Ich sehe, du trägst nicht schwer an deinen Sorgen.«

2.4

I see you are not heavy with your troubles."

»Was soll ich traurig sein.«

2.5

"Why should I be sad."

antwortete der Knecht, »ich habe vollauf, der Lohn von drei Jahren klingelt in meiner Tasche.«

2.6

replied the servant, "I have my fill; three years' wages are ringing in my pocket."

»Wieviel ist denn deines Schatzes?« fragte ihn das Männchen.

2.7

"How much is your treasure?" the little man asked him.

»Wieviel? Drei bare Heller, richtig gezählt.«

2.8

"How much? Three hard pennies, counted correctly."

»Höre.« sagte der Zwerg,

2.9

"Listen." said the dwarf,

»ich bin ein armer, bedürftiger Mann, schenke mir deine drei Heller:

2.10

"I am a poor, needy man, give me your three pennies:

ich kann nichts mehr arbeiten,

2.11

I can't do any more work,

164

2.12 du aber bist jung und kannst dir dein Brot leicht verdienen.«

but you are young and can earn your bread easily."

2.13 Und weil der Knecht ein gutes Herz hatte und Mitleid mit dem Männchen fühlte, so reichte er ihm seine drei Heller, und sprach,

And because the servant had a good heart and felt pity for the little man, he gave him his three pennies and said,

2.14 »In Gottes Namen, es wird mir doch nicht fehlen.«

"In God's name, I will not want for anything."

2.15 Da sprach das Männchen:

Then the little man said,

2.16 »Weil ich dein gutes Herz sehe, so gewähre ich dir drei Wünsche, für jeden Heller einen, die sollen dir in Erfüllung gehen.«

"Because I see your good heart, I will grant you three wishes, one for every penny, and they shall come true."

2.17 »Aha.« sprach der Knecht,

"Ah." said the servant,

2.18 »du bist einer, der blau pfeifen kann.

"you are one who can whistle blue.

2.19 Wohlan, wenn's doch sein soll, so wünsche ich mir erstlich ein Vogelrohr, das alles trifft, wonach ich ziele;

Well, if it is to be, I wish, first of all, a fowler's pipe, which will hit everything I aim at;

zweitens eine Fiedel, wenn ich darauf streiche, so 2.20
muß alles tanzen, was den Klang hört;
secondly, a fiddle, when I strike it, everything that hears
the sound must dance;

und drittens, wenn ich an jemand eine Bitte thue, so 2.21
darf er sie nicht abschlagen.«
and thirdly, if I make a request of any one, he must not
refuse it."

»Das sollst du alles haben.« 2.22
"You shall have all this."

sprach das Männchen, griff in den Busch, und 2.23
denk einer, da lag schon Fiedel und Vogelrohr in
Bereitschaft, als wenn sie bestellt wären.
said the little man, reaching into the bush, and think of it,
there lay the fiddle and the bird's reed in readiness, as if
they had been ordered.

Er gab sie dem Knecht und sprach, 2.24
He gave them to the servant and said,

»Was du dir immer erbitten wirst, 2.25
"Whatever you ask for,

kein Mensch auf der Welt soll dir's abschlagen.« 2.26
no one in the world shall refuse you."

»Herz, was begehrst du nun?« 3.1
"Heart, what do you want now?"

sprach der Knecht zu sich selber und zog lustig 3.2
weiter.
said the servant to himself and went on his merry way.

3.3 Bald darauf begegnete er einem Juden mit einem langen Ziegenbart, der stand und horchte auf den Gesang eines Vogels, der hoch oben in der Spitze eines Baumes saß.

Soon afterwards he met a Jew with a long goatee, who stood listening to the song of a bird perched high up in the top of a tree.

3.4 »Gottes Wunder!« rief er aus,

"God's wonder!" he exclaimed,

3.5 »so ein kleines Tier hat so eine grausam mächtige Stimme!

"such a small animal has such a cruelly powerful voice!

3.6 Wenn's doch mein wäre!

If only it were mine!

3.7 Wer ihm doch Salz auf den Schwanz streuen könnte!«

Who could sprinkle salt on its tail!"

3.8 »Wenn's weiter nichts ist.« sprach der Knecht,

"If it's nothing else." said the servant,

3.9 »der Vogel soll bald herunter sein.«

"the bird shall soon be down."

3.10 legte an und traf auf's Haar,

He struck it on the hair,

3.11 und der Vogel fiel herab in die Dornhecken. »Geh,

and the bird fell down into the thorn-hedges. "Go,

3.12 Spitzbub.« sagte er zum Juden,

rogue." he said to the Jew,

»und hol dir den Vogel heraus.«   3.13
"and get the bird out for yourself."

»Mein.« sprach der Jude, »laß der Herr den Bub weg,   3.14
"My dear." said the Jew, "if the master lets the boy go,

so kommt ein Hund gelaufen; ich will mir den Vogel   3.15
auflesen,
a dog will come running; I will pick up the bird,

weil Ihr ihn doch einmal getroffen habt.«   3.16
because you have hit it once."

legte sich auf die Erde und fing an sich in den Busch   3.17
hinein zu arbeiten.
He lay down on the ground and began to work his way into
the bush.

Wie er nun mitten in dem Dorn steckte, plagte der   3.18
Mutwille den guten Knecht, daß er seine Fiedel
abnahm und anfing zu geigen.
As he was now in the midst of the thorn, the good servant
was so plagued with courage that he took down his fiddle
and began to fiddle.

Gleich fing auch der Jude an die Beine zu heben und   3.19
in die Höhe zu springen, und je mehr der Knecht
strich, desto besser ging der Tanz.
Immediately the Jew also began to lift his legs and jump up
into the air, and the more the servant stroked, the better
the dance went.

Aber die Dornen zerrissen ihm den schäbigen Rock,   3.20
But the thorns tore his shabby skirt,

kämmten ihm den Ziegenbart und stachen und   3.21
zwickten ihn am ganzen Leib.
combed his goatee and stung and pinched him all over.

3.22 »Mein.« rief der Jude, »was soll mir das Geigen!
"My." cried the Jew, "what's the use of fiddling!

3.23 Laß der Herr das Geigen, ich begehre nicht zu tanzen.«
Let the Lord leave the violin, I don't want to dance."

3.24 Aber der Knecht hörte nicht darauf und dachte,
But the servant paid no attention, and thought,

3.25 »Du hast die Leute genug geschunden,
"You have maltreated the people enough,

3.26 nun soll dir's die Dornenhecke nicht besser machen.«
now the thorn hedge shall not do you any better."

3.27 und fing von neuem an zu geigen, daß der Jude immer höher aufspringen mußte, und die Fetzen von seinem Rock an den Stacheln hängen blieben.
and began to fiddle again, so that the Jew had to jump up higher and higher, and the shreds of his skirt caught on the thorns.

3.28 »Au weih geschrien!« rief der Jude,
"Oh, dear!" cried the Jew,

3.29 »geb ich doch dem Herrn, was er verlangt, wenn er nur das Geigen läßt, einen ganzen Beutel mit Gold.«
"I'll give the master what he wants, if he'll only let me play the violin, a whole bag of gold."

3.30 »Wenn du so spendabel bist.« sprach der Knecht,
"If you are so generous." said the servant,

»so will ich wohl mit meiner Musik aufhören, aber
das muß ich dir nachrühmen, du machst deinen Tanz
noch mit, daß es eine Art hat.«

3.31

"I will stop my music, but I must tell you that you are still
doing your dance, so that it is something."

nahm darauf den Beutel und ging seiner Wege.

3.32

Then he took the bag and went his way.

Der Jude blieb stehen und sah ihm nach und war still
bis der Knecht weit weg und ihm ganz aus den Augen
war, dann schrie er aus Leibeskräften:

4.1

The Jew stopped and looked after him, and was silent
till the servant was far away and out of his sight, then he
shouted at the top of his voice,

»Du miserabler Musikant, du Bierfiedler, wart, wenn
ich dich allein erwische!

4.2

"You miserable musician, you beer-fiddler, wait till I catch
you alone!

Ich will dich jagen, daß du die Schuhsohlen verlieren
sollst, du Lump;

4.3

I will hunt you down so that you shall lose the soles of your
shoes, you rascal;

steck einen Groschen ins Maul, daß du sechs Heller
wert bist.«

4.4

put a penny in your mouth so that you are worth six
farthings."

und schimpfte weiter, was er nur losbringen konnte.

4.5

and went on ranting as much as he could get away with.

4.6 **Und als er sich damit etwas zu gute gethan und Luft gemacht hatte,**

And when he had done himself some good and given vent to it,

4.7 **lief er in die Stadt zum Richter. »Herr Richter,**

he ran into the town to the judge. "Mr. Judge,

4.8 **au weih geschrien!**

oh my!

4.9 **Seht wie mich auf offener Landstraße ein gottloser Mensch beraubt und übel zugerichtet hat,**

See how a wicked man has robbed and maltreated me in the open country,

4.10 **ein Stein auf dem Erdboden möcht sich erbarmen:**

a stone on the ground would have mercy:

4.11 **die Kleider zerfetzt! der Leib zerstochen und zerkratzt!**

my clothes torn to shreds! my body stung and scratched!

4.12 **mein bißchen Armut samt dem Beutel genommen!**

my little poverty taken with my purse!

4.13 **lauter Dukaten, ein Stück schöner als das andere, um Gottes willen, laßt den Menschen ins Gefängnis werfen.«**

all my ducats, one piece more beautiful than the other, for God's sake, let the man be thrown into prison."

4.14 **Sprach der Richter:**

Said the Judge,

»War's ein Soldat, der dich mit seinem Säbel so
zugerichtet hat?«
"Was it a soldier who has so maltreated you with his
sabre?"

4.15

»Gott bewahre!« sagte der Jude,
"God forbid!" said the Jew,

4.16

»einen nackten Degen hat er nicht gehabt,
"he did not have a naked sword,

4.17

aber ein Rohr hat er gehabt auf dem Buckel hängen
und eine Geige am Hals;
but he had a reed hanging on his hump and a violin on his
neck;

4.18

der Bösewicht ist leicht zu erkennen.«
the villain is easy to recognize."

4.19

Der Richter schickte seine Leute nach ihm aus, die
fanden den guten Knecht, der ganz langsam weiter
gezogen war, und fanden auch den Beutel mit Gold
bei ihm.
The judge sent his men after him, who found the good
servant, who had moved on very slowly, and also found the
bag of gold with him.

4.20

Als er vor Gericht gestellt wurde, sagte er:
When he was put on trial, he said:

4.21

»Ich habe den Juden nicht angerührt und ihm
das Geld nicht genommen, er hat mir's aus freien
Stücken angeboten, damit ich nur aufhörte zu geigen,
weil er meine Musik nicht vertragen konnte.«
"I didn't touch the Jew and didn't take the money from
him, he offered it to me of his own free will so that I
would stop playing the violin because he couldn't stand
my music."

4.22

4.23 »Gott bewahre!« schrie der Jude,
"God forbid!" cried the Jew,

4.24 »der greift die Lügen wie Fliegen an der Wand.«
"he picks up lies like flies on the wall."

4.25 Aber der Richter glaubte es auch nicht und sprach,
But the judge did not believe it either and said,

4.26 »Das ist eine schlechte Entschuldigung, das thut kein Jude.«
"That is a poor excuse, no Jew would do that."

4.27 und verurteilte den guten Knecht, weil er auf offener Straße einen Raub begangen hätte, zum Galgen.
and sentenced the good servant to the gallows because he had committed a robbery in the open street.

4.28 Als er aber abgeführt ward, schrie ihm noch der Jude zu:
But as he was being led away, the Jew shouted to him:

4.29 »Du Bärenhäuter, du Hundemusikant, jetzt kriegst du deinen wohlverdienten Lohn.«
"You bearskinner, you dog-musician, now you'll get your well-deserved reward."

4.30 Der Knecht stieg ganz ruhig mit dem Henker die Leiter hinauf,
The servant calmly climbed up the ladder with the executioner,

4.31 auf der letzten Sprosse aber drehte er sich um und sprach zum Richter:
but on the last rung he turned around and said to the judge:

4.32 »Gewährt mir noch eine Bitte, ehe ich sterbe.«
"Grant me one more request before I die."

»Ja.« sprach der Richter,   4.33
"Yes." said the judge,

»wenn du nicht um dein Leben bittest.«   4.34
"if you don't ask for your life."

»Nicht ums Leben.« antwortete der Knecht,   4.35
"Not for my life." replied the servant,

»ich bitte, laßt mich zuguterletzt noch einmal auf   4.36
meiner Geige spielen.«
"I beg you to let me play my violin one last time."

Der Jude erhob ein Zetergeschrei: 4.37
The Jew raised a clamor:

»Um Gottes willen, erlaubt's nicht, erlaubt's nicht.«   4.38
"For God's sake, don't allow it, don't allow it."

Allein der Richter sprach: 4.39
But the judge said:

»Warum soll ich ihm die kurze Freude nicht gönnen: 4.40
"Why shouldn't I grant him this brief pleasure:

es ist ihm zugestanden, und dabei soll es sein   4.41
Bewenden haben.«
it's granted to him and that's the end of it."

Auch konnte er es ihm nicht abschlagen wegen der   4.42
Gabe, die dem Knecht verliehen war.
Nor could he refuse him because of the gift that had been
given to the servant.

Der Jude aber rief: »Au weih! au weih! bindet   4.43
mich an,
But the Jew cried out: "Oh my! oh my! bind me,

4.44 bindet mich fest.«

bind me tightly."

4.45 Da nahm der gute Knecht seine Geige vom Halse,
legte sie zurecht, und wie er den ersten Strich that,
fing alles an zu wabern und zu wanken, der Richter,
die Schreiber und die Gerichtsdiener, und der Strick
fiel dem aus der Hand, der den Juden festbinden
wollte;

Then the good servant took his violin from his neck, put it
to rights, and as he struck the first stroke, everything began
to shake and sway, the judge, the scribes, and the officers of
the court, and the rope fell from the hand of him who was
going to bind the Jew;

4.46 beim, zweiten Strich hoben alle die Beine, und der
Henker ließ den guten Knecht los und machte sich
zum Tanze fertig;

at the second stroke they all lifted their legs, and the
executioner let go the good servant and prepared to dance;

4.47 bei dem dritten Strich sprang alles in die Höhe und
fing an zu tanzen,

at the third stroke they all jumped up and began to dance,

4.48 und der Richter und der Jude waren vorn und
sprangen am besten.

and the judge and the Jew were in front and jumped the
best.

4.49 Bald tanzte alles mit, was auf den Markt aus
Neugierde herbeigekommen war, alte und junge,
dicke und magere Leute untereinander;

Soon everyone who had come to the market out of curiosity
was dancing along, old and young, fat and skinny people
among themselves;

sogar die Hunde, die mitgelaufen waren, setzten sich auf die Hinterfüße und hüpften mit. 4.50

even the dogs that had run along sat on their hind feet and jumped along.

Und je länger er spielte, desto höher sprangen die Tänzer, daß sie sich einander an die Köpfe stießen und anfingen jämmerlich zu schreien. 4.51

And the longer he played, the higher the dancers jumped, so that they bumped into each other's heads and began to scream miserably.

Endlich rief der Richter ganz außer Atem: 4.52

At last the judge called out, quite out of breath:

»Ich schenke dir dein Leben, höre nur auf zu geigen.« 4.53

"I'll give you your life, just stop playing the violin."

Der gute Knecht ließ sich bewegen, setzte die Geige ab, hing sie wieder um den Hals und stieg die Leiter herab. 4.54

The good servant was moved, put down the violin, hung it around his neck again and climbed down the ladder.

Da trat er zu dem Juden, der auf der Erde lag und nach Atem schnappte und sagte: 4.55

Then he approached the Jew, who was lying on the ground gasping for breath, and said,

»Spitzbube, jetzt gesteh, wo du das Geld her hast, oder ich nehme meine Geige vom Halse und fange wieder an zu spielen.« 4.56

"Rascal, now confess where you got the money, or I'll take my violin off my neck and start playing again."

»Ich hab's gestohlen, ich hab's gestohlen.« schrie er, 4.57

"I stole it, I stole it." he shouted,

4.58 »du aber hast's redlich verdient.«

"but you earned it fair and square."

4.59 Da ließ der Richter den Juden zum Galgen führen und als einen Dieb aufhängen.

So the judge had the Jew led to the gallows and hanged as a thief.

Der gelernte Jäger

The Skilled Hunter

1.1 Es war einmal ein junger Bursch, der hatte die Schlosserhantierung gelernt und sprach zu seinem Vater, er wollte jetzt in die Welt gehen und sich versuchen.

Once upon a time there was a young lad who had learned to be a locksmith and said to his father that he now wanted to go out into the world and try his hand.

1.2 »Ja.« sagte der Vater, »das bin ich zufrieden.«

"Yes." said his father, "I'm happy to do that."

1.3 und gab ihm etwas Geld auf die Reise.

and gave him some money for the journey.

1.4 Also zog er herum und suchte Arbeit.

So he went around looking for work.

1.5 Auf eine Zeit, da wollte ihm das Schlosserwerk nicht mehr folgen und stand ihm auch nicht mehr an, aber er kriegte Lust zur Jägerei.

At one point, the locksmith's shop no longer wanted to follow him and no longer suited him, but he took a fancy to hunting.

Da begegnete ihm auf der Wanderschaft ein Jäger in 1.6
grünem Kleide, der fragte, wo er her käme und wo er
hin wollte.
On his wanderings, he met a hunter in green, who asked
where he came from and where he was going.

Er wäre ein Schlossergesell, sagte der Bursch, aber 1.7
das Handwerk gefiele ihm nicht mehr, und er hätte
Lust zur Jägerei, ob er ihn als Lehrling annehmen
wollte.
He was a journeyman locksmith, said the lad, but he no
longer liked the trade and wanted to go hunting, so he
asked if he would take him on as an apprentice.

»O ja, wenn du mit mir gehen willst.« 1.8
"Oh yes, if you want to go with me."

Da ging der junge Bursch mit, 1.9
So the young lad went with him,

vermietete sich etliche Jahre bei ihm und lernte die 1.10
Jägerei.
hired himself out to him for several years and learned to
hunt.

Danach wollte er sich weiter versuchen, und der 1.11
Jäger gab ihm nichts zum Lohn als eine Windbüchse,
die hatte aber die Eigenschaft, wenn er damit einen
Schuß that, so traf er unfehlbar.
Afterwards he wanted to try his hand at it, and the
huntsman gave him nothing for wages but a wind rifle,
which, however, had the property that when he made a
shot with it, he hit it unerringly.

1.12 Da ging er fort und kam in einen sehr großen Wald, von dem konnte er in einem Tage das Ende nicht finden.

So he went away, and came to a very large forest, from which he could not find the end in a day.

1.13 Wie's Abend war, setzte er sich auf einen hohen Baum, damit er aus dem Bereich der wilden Tiere käme.

As it was evening, he sat down on a high tree, that he might get out of the reach of the wild beasts.

1.14 Gegen Mitternacht zu, deuchte ihm, schimmerte ein kleines Lichtchen von weitem, da sah er durch die Äste darauf hin und behielt in acht, wo es war.

Towards midnight, it seemed to him, a small light shimmered from afar, so he looked at it through the branches and took care where it was.

1.15 Doch nahm er erst noch seinen Hut und warf ihn nach dem Licht zu herunter, daß er danach gehen wollte, wann er herabgestiegen wäre, als nach einem Zeichen.

But first he took his hat and threw it down towards the light, so that he could see when he had descended, as if by a sign.

1.16 Nun kletterte er herunter, ging auf seinen Hut los, setzte ihn wieder auf und zog geradeswegs fort.

Now he climbed down, went for his hat, put it on again, and went straight on.

Je weiter er ging, desto größer ward das Lichts und wie er nahe herbei kam, sah er, daß es ein gewaltiges Feuer war, und saßen drei Riesen dabei und hatten einen Ochsen am Spieß und ließen ihn braten.

1.17

The farther he went, the greater the light grew, and as he drew near he saw that it was a mighty fire, and three giants were sitting by it, and had an ox on a spit, and were roasting it.

Nun sprach der eine:

1.18

Now one of them said,

»Ich muß doch schmecken, ob das Fleisch bald zu essen ist.«

1.19

"I must taste whether the meat will soon be ready to eat."

riß ein Stück herab und wollte es in den Mund stecken,

1.20

He tore off a piece and wanted to put it into his mouth,

aber der Jäger schoß es ihm aus der Hand. »Nun ja.«

1.21

but the huntsman shot it out of his hand. "Well."

sprach der Riese,

1.22

said the giant,

»da weht mir der Wind das Stück aus der Hand.«

1.23

"the wind is blowing the piece out of my hand."

und nahm sich ein anderes. Wie er eben anbeißen wollte,

1.24

and he took another. Just as he was about to take a bite,

schoß es ihm der Jäger abermals weg;

1.25

the hunter shot it away again;

1.26 da gab der Riese dem, der neben ihm saß, eine
Ohrfeige und rief zornig,
then the giant slapped the man sitting next to him and
shouted angrily,

1.27 »Was reißt du mir mein Stück weg?«
"Why are you tearing my piece away?"

1.28 »Ich habe es nicht weggerissen.« sprach der andere,
"I didn't tear it away." said the other,

1.29 »es wird dir's ein Scharfschütze weggeschossen
haben.«
"a sharpshooter must have shot it away."

1.30 Der Riese nahm sich das dritte Stück, konnte es aber
nicht in der Hand behalten, der Jäger schoß es ihm
heraus.
The giant took the third piece, but could not keep it in his
hand; the hunter shot it out of his hand.

1.31 Da sprachen die Riesen:
Then the giants said,

1.32 »Das muß ein guter Schütze sein, der den Bissen vor
dem Maul wegschießt, so einer wär uns nützlich.«
"That must be a good marksman who shoots the morsel
away from his mouth, such a one would be useful to us."

1.33 und riefen laut:
and cried aloud,

1.34 »Komm herbei, du Scharfschütze, setze dich zu uns
ans Feuer und iß dich satt, wir wollen dir nichts
thun;
"Come here, you sharpshooter, sit down by the fire and eat
your fill, we will do you no harm;

aber kommst du nicht, und wir holen dich mit
Gewalt, so bist du verloren.«

but if you do not come, and we take you by force, you are
lost."

Da trat der Bursche herzu und sagte, er wäre ein
gelernter Jäger, und wonach er mit seiner Büchse
ziele, das treffe er auch sicher und gewiß.

Then the lad came up and said that he was a skilled hunter,
and that whatever he aimed at with his rifle he would
certainly hit.

Da sprachen sie, wenn er mit ihnen gehen wollte,
sollte er's gut haben, und erzählten ihm, vor dem
Walde sei ein großes Wasser, dahinter stände
ein Turm, und in dem Turm säße eine schöne
Königstochter, die wollten sie gern rauben.

Then they said that if he would go with them, he should
have a good time, and told him that there was a large
body of water in front of the forest, behind which stood
a tower, and in the tower sat a beautiful princess, whom
they wished to steal.

»Ja.« sprach er, »die will ich bald geschafft haben.«

"Yes." he said, "I want to get her soon."

Sagten sie weiter:

They continued,

»Es ist aber noch etwas dabei, es liegt ein kleines
Hündchen dort, das fängt gleich an zu bellen, wenn
sich jemand nähert, und sobald das bellt, wacht auch
alles am königlichen Hofe auf, und deshalb können
wir nicht hineinkommen;

"But there is something else, there is a little dog lying there,
which begins to bark as soon as anyone approaches, and
as soon as it barks, everything in the royal court wakes up,
and that is why we cannot get in;

1.41 getraust du dich das Hündchen tot zu schießen?«
do you dare to shoot the dog dead?"

1.42 »Ja.« sprach er, »das ist mir ein kleiner Spaß.«
"Yes." he said, "that's a bit of fun for me."

1.43 Danach setzte er sich auf ein Schiff und fuhr über das
Wasser, und wie er bald beim Lande war, kam das
Hündlein gelaufen und wollte bellen, aber er kriegte
seine Windbüchse und schoß es tot.
Then he got on a boat and sailed across the water, and when
he was soon on shore, the little dog came running and
wanted to bark, but he got his wind rifle and shot it dead.

1.44 Wie die Riesen das sahen, freuten sie sich und
meinten, sie hätten die Königstochter schon gewiß,
aber der Jäger wollte erst sehen, wie die Sache
beschaffen war und sprach, sie sollten haußen
bleiben, bis er sie riefe.
When the giants saw this, they rejoiced, and thought they
had already got the King's daughter for certain, but the
huntsman first wanted to see how things were, and told
them to stay outside until he called them.

1.45 Da ging er in das Schloß, und es war mäuschenstill
darin und schlief alles.
So he went into the castle, and it was as quiet as a mouse,
and all was asleep.

1.46 Wie er das erste Zimmer aufmachte, hing da ein
Säbel an der Wand, der war von purem Silber und
war ein goldener Stern darauf und des Königs Name;
When he opened the first room, there hung on the wall a
sabre of pure silver, with a golden star on it and the King's
name;

daneben aber lag auf einem Tisch ein versiegelter Brief, den brach er auf, und es stand darin, wer den Säbel hätte, könnte alles ums Leben bringen, was ihm vorkäme.

1.47

and beside it on a table lay a sealed letter, which he broke open, and it said that whoever had the sabre could kill anything that came before him.

Da nahm er den Säbel von der Wand, hing ihn um und ging weiter;

1.48

So he took the sabre from the wall, hung it round him, and went on his way;

da kam er in das Zimmer, wo die Königstochter lag und schlief, und sie war so schön, daß er still stand und sie betrachtete und den Atem anhielt.

1.49

then he came into the room where the King's daughter lay sleeping, and she was so beautiful that he stood still and looked at her and held his breath.

Er dachte bei sich selbst:

1.50

He thought to himself,

»Wie darf ich eine unschuldige Jungfrau in die Gewalt der wilden Riesen bringen,

1.51

"How can I bring an innocent maiden into the power of the wild giants,

die haben Böses im Sinn.«

1.52

they have evil in mind."

Er schaute sich weiter um, da standen unter dem Bett ein Paar Pantoffeln, auf dem rechten stand ihres Vaters Name mit einem Stern und auf dem linken ihr eigener Name mit einem Stern.

1.53

He continued to look around, there were a pair of slippers under the bed, on the right one was her father's name with a star and on the left one her own name with a star.

186

1.54 Sie hatte auch ein großes Halstuch um, von Seide mit Gold ausgestickt, auf der rechten Seite ihres Vaters Name, auf der linken ihr Name, alles mit goldenen Buchstaben.

She also had a large scarf round her neck, made of silk embroidered with gold, with her father's name on the right and her own name on the left, all in gold letters.

1.55 Da nahm der Jäger eine Schere, und schnitt den rechten Schlippen ab und that ihn in seinen Ranzen, und dann nahm er auch den rechten Pantoffel mit des Königs Namen und steckte ihn hinein.

Then the huntsman took a pair of scissors, and cut off the right hand scarf, and put it into his satchel, and then he took the right hand slipper with the King's name on it, and put it in.

1.56 Nun lag die Jungfrau noch immer und schlief, und sie war ganz in ihr Hemd eingenäht: da schnitt er auch ein Stückchen von dem Hemd ab und steckte es zu dem anderen, doch that er das alles ohne sie anzurühren.

Now the maiden was still lying and sleeping, and she was all sewn up in her shirt, so he cut off a piece of the shirt and put it in with the other, but he did all this without touching her.

1.57 Dann ging er fort und ließ sie ungestört schlafen, und als er wieder ans Thor kam, standen die Riesen noch draußen, warteten auf ihn und dachten, er würde die Königstochter bringen.

Then he went away and left her to sleep undisturbed, and when he came back to the gate the giants were still standing outside waiting for him, thinking that he would bring the King's daughter.

Er rief ihnen aber zu, sie sollten hereinkommen, die 1.58
Jungfrau wäre schon in seiner Gewalt;
But he called to them to come in, the maiden was already in
his power;

die Thür könnte er ihnen aber nicht aufmachen, 1.59
aber da wäre ein Loch, durch welches sie kriechen
müßten.
he could not open the door for them, but there was a hole
through which they would have to crawl.

Nun kam der erste näher, da wickelte, der Jäger des 1.60
Riesen Haar um seine Hand, zog den Kopf herein und
hieb ihn mit seinem Säbel in einem Streich ab, und
zog ihn dann vollends hinein.
Now the first came nearer, and the huntsman wrapped
the giant's hair round his hand, pulled his head in and cut
it off with his sabre in one stroke, and then pulled him in
completely.

Dann rief er den zweiten und hieb ihm gleichfalls das 1.61
Haupt ab, und endlich auch dem dritten, und war
froh, daß er die schöne Jungfrau von ihren Feinden
befreit hatte, und schnitt ihnen die Zungen aus und
steckte sie in seinen Ranzen.
Then he called the second and cut off his head likewise,
and finally the third also, and was glad that he had freed
the beautiful maiden from her enemies, and cut out their
tongues and put them in his satchel.

Da dachte er: 1.62
Then he thought,

»Ich will heimgehen zu meinem Vater und ihm 1.63
zeigen, was ich schon gethan habe, dann will ich
in der Welt herumziehen;
"I will go home to my father, and show him what I have
already done, and then I will go about the world;

1.64 das Glück, das mir Gott bescheren will, wird mich schon erreichen.«

the happiness which God wants to give me will reach me."

2.1 Der König in dem Schloß aber, als er aufwachte, erblickte er die drei Riesen, die da tot lagen.

But when the king woke up in the castle, he saw the three giants lying there dead.

2.2 Dann ging er in die Schlafkammer seiner Tochter, weckte sie auf und fragte, wer das wohl gewesen wäre, der die Riesen ums Leben gebracht hätte.

Then he went into his daughter's bedchamber, woke her up and asked who had killed the giants.

2.3 Da sagte sie,

She said,

2.4 »Lieber Vater, ich weiß es nicht, ich habe geschlafen.«

"Dear father, I don't know, I was asleep."

2.5 Wie sie nun aufstand und ihre Pantoffeln anziehen wollte, da war der rechte weg, und wie sie ihr Halstuch betrachtete, war es durchschnitten und fehlte der rechte Schlippen, und wie sie ihr Hemd ansah, war ein Stückchen heraus.

When she got up and went to put on her slippers, the right one was gone, and when she looked at her kerchief, it was cut through, and the right lip was missing, and when she looked at her shirt, a piece was out.

2.6 Der König ließ den ganzen Hof zusammenkommen, Soldaten und alles was da war und fragte, wer seine Tochter befreit und die Riesen ums Leben gebracht hätte?

The king summoned the whole court, soldiers and all, and asked who had freed his daughter and killed the giants?

Nun hatte er einen Hauptmann, der war einäugig
und ein häßlicher Mensch, der sagte, er hätte es
gethan.

2.7

Now he had a captain who was one-eyed and an ugly man,
who said that he had done it.

Da sprach der alte König, so er das vollbracht hätte,
sollte er seine Tochter auch heiraten.

2.8

Then the old king said that if he had done it, he should
marry his daughter.

Die Jungfrau aber sagte:

2.9

But the maiden said,

»Lieber Vater, dafür, daß ich den heiraten soll, will
ich lieber in die Welt gehen, so weit als mich meine
Beine tragen.«

2.10

"Dear father, I would rather go into the world as far as my
legs will carry me, if I am to marry him."

Da sprach der König, wenn sie den nicht heiraten
wollte, sollte sie die königlichen Kleider ausziehen
und Bauernkleider anthun und fortgehen; und sie
sollte zu einem Töpfer gehen und einen Handel mit
irdenem Geschirr anfangen.

2.11

Then the King said, if she would not marry him, she should
take off her royal garments and put on peasant's clothes and
go away, and she should go to a potter and begin a trade in
earthenware.

Da that sie ihre königlichen Kleider aus und ging
zu einem Töpfer und borgte sich einen Kram irden
Werk, sie versprach ihm auch, wenn sie es am Abend
verkauft hätte, wollte sie es bezahlen.

2.12

So she took off her royal clothes and went to a potter and
borrowed a piece of earthenware, and promised him that if
she sold it that evening she would pay for it.

2.13 Nun sagte der König, sie sollte sich an eine Ecke damit setzen und es verkaufen.

Now the king told her to sit down on a corner and sell it.

2.14 Dann bestellte er etliche Bauernwagen, die sollten mitten durchfahren, daß alles in tausend Stucke ginge.

Then he ordered a number of peasant carts to drive through the middle, so that everything would go in a thousand pieces.

2.15 Wie nun die Königstochter ihren Kram auf die Straße hingestellt hatte,

As soon as the King's daughter had placed her things in the street,

2.16 kamen die Wagen und zerbrachen ihn zu lauter Scherben.

the carts came and broke them to pieces.

2.17 Sie fing an zu weinen und sprach,

She began to weep, and said,

2.18 »Ach Gott, wie will ich nun dem Töpfer bezahlen.«

"Oh, God, how will I pay the potter now."

2.19 Der König aber hatte sie damit zwingen wollen, den Hauptmann zu heiraten, statt dessen ging sie wieder zum Töpfer und fragte ihn, ob er ihr noch einmal borgen wollte.

The king had wanted to force her to marry the captain, but instead she went back to the potter and asked him if he wanted to lend to her again.

2.20 Er antwortete nein, sie sollte erst das vorige bezahlen.

He replied no, she should pay the previous one first.

Da ging sie zu ihrem Vater, schrie und jammerte und sagte, sie wollte in die Welt hineingehen.

2.21

Then she went to her father, cried and wailed and said she wanted to go into the world.

Da sprach er:

2.22

Then he said,

»Ich will dir draußen in dem Walde ein Häuschen bauen lassen, darin sollst du dein Lebtag sitzen und für jedermann kochen, du darfst aber kein Geld nehmen.«

2.23

"I will have a little house built for you out in the forest, and you shall sit in it all your life and cook for everyone, but you must not take any money."

Als das Häuschen fertig war, ward vor die Thür ein Schild gehängt, darauf stand geschrieben,

2.24

When the cottage was finished, a sign was hung outside the door, on which was written,

»Heute umsonst, morgen für Geld.«

2.25

"Today for nothing, tomorrow for money."

Da saß sie lange Zeit, und sprach es sich in der Welt herum, da säße eine Jungfrau, die kochte umsonst, und das stände vor der Thür an einem Schild.

2.26

There she sat for a long time, and word spread through the world that there was a maiden who cooked for nothing, and that this was written on a sign outside the door.

Das hörte auch der Jäger und dachte,

2.27

The hunter heard this too, and thought,

»Das wär etwas für dich,

2.28

"That would be something for you,

2.29 du bist doch arm und hast kein Geld.«

you are poor and have no money."

2.30 Er nahm also seine Windbüchse und den Ranzen, worin noch alles steckte, was er damals im Schloß als Wahrzeichen mitgenommen hatte, ging in den Wald und fand auch das Häuschen mit dem Schild:

So he took his wind rifle and his satchel, which still contained everything he had taken with him from the castle as a symbol, went into the forest and found the little house with the sign:

2.31 »Heute umsonst, morgen für Geld.«

"Today for free, tomorrow for money."

2.32 Er hatte aber den Degen umhängen, womit er den drei Riesen den Kopf abgehauen hatte, trat so in das Häuschen hinein und ließ sich etwas zu essen geben.

But he had the sword around his neck with which he had cut off the heads of the three giants, so he entered the cottage and asked for something to eat.

2.33 Er freute sich über das schöne Mädchen, es, war aber auch bildschön.

He was pleased to see the beautiful girl, but she was also beautiful.

2.34 Sie fragte, wo er her käme und hin wollte, da sägte er,

She asked him where he had come from and where he was going, and he said,

2.35 »Ich reise in der Welt herum.«

"I'm traveling around the world."

Da fragte sie ihn, wo er den Degen her hätte, da
stände ja ihres Vaters Name darauf.

2.36

Then she asked him where he had gotten the sword, as it
had her father's name on it.

Fragte er, ob sie des Königs Tochter wäre. »Ja.«

2.37

He asked if she was the king's daughter. "Yes."

antwortete sie. »Mit diesem Säbel.« sprach er,

2.38

she answered. "With this sabre." he said,

»habe ich drei Riesen den Kopf abgehauen.«

2.39

"I have cut off the heads of three giants."

und holte zum Zeichen ihre Zungen aus dem Ranzen,
dann zeigte er ihr auch den Pantoffel, den Schlippen
vom Halstuch und das Stück vom Hemd.

2.40

and took her tongues out of her satchel as a sign, and then
he showed her the slipper, the sliver of the scarf, and the
piece of the shirt.

Da war sie voll Freude und sagte, er wäre derjenige,
der sie erlöst hätte.

2.41

She was full of joy and said that he was the one who had
redeemed her.

Darauf gingen sie zusammen zum alten König und
holten ihn herbei, und sie führte ihn in ihre Kammer
und sagte ihm, der Jäger wäre der rechte, der sie von
den Riesen erlöst hätte.

2.42

Then they went together to the old king and fetched him,
and she led him into her chamber and told him that the
huntsman was the one who had delivered her from the
giants.

2.43 Und wie der alte König die Wahrzeichen alle sah, da konnte er nicht mehr zweifeln und sagte, es wäre ihm lieb, daß er wüßte wie alles zugegangen wäre, und er sollte sie nun auch zur Gemahlin haben; darüber freute sich die Jungfrau von Herzen.

And when the old King saw all the signs, he could doubt no longer, and said that he would be glad to know how everything had happened, and that he should now have her for his wife, and the maiden was heartily glad of it.

2.44 Darauf kleideten sie ihn, als wenn er ein fremder Herr wäre, und der König ließ ein Gastmahl anstellen.

Then they dressed him as if he were a stranger, and the King ordered a banquet to be served.

2.45 Als sie nun zu Tisch gingen, kam der Hauptmann auf die linke Seite der Königstochter zu sitzen, der Jäger aber auf die rechte, und der Hauptmann meinte, das wäre ein fremder Herr und wäre zum Besuch gekommen.

Now when they went to table, the captain came to sit on the left side of the king's daughter, and the huntsman on the right, and the captain thought he was a strange gentleman, and had come to visit her.

2.46 Wie sie gegessen und getrunken hatten, sprach der alte König zum Hauptmann, er wollte ihm etwas aufgeben, das sollte er erraten:

When they had eaten and drunk, the old king said to the captain that he would give him something to guess:

wenn einer spräche, er hätte drei Riesen ums Leben gebracht, und er gefragt würde, wo die Zungen der Riesen wären, und er müßte zusehen und wären keine in ihren Köpfen, wie dies zuginge?   2.47

if one of them said he had killed three giants, and he was asked where the giants' tongues were, and he had to watch, and there were none in their heads, how would this happen?

Da sagte der Hauptmann: »Sie werden keine gehabt haben.«   2.48

Then the captain said, "They will not have had any."

»Nicht so.« sagte der König, »jedes Getier hat eine Zunge.«   2.49

"Not so." said the king, "every beast has a tongue."

und fragte weiter, was der wert wäre, daß ihm widerführe?   2.50

and asked further, what was it worth that it should happen to him?

Antwortete der Hauptmann,   2.51

The captain replied,

»Der gehört in Stücke zerrissen zu werden!«   2.52

"He ought to be torn to pieces!"

Da sagte der König, er hätte sich selber sein Urteil gesprochen, und ward der Hauptmann gefänglich gesetzt und dann in vier Stücke zerrissen, die Königstochter aber mit dem Jäger vermählt.   2.53

Then the king said that he had pronounced his own judgment, and the captain was imprisoned and then torn in four pieces, but the king's daughter was married to the huntsman.

2.54 Danach holte er seinen Vater und seine Mutter
herbei, und die lebten in Freude bei ihrem Sohn,
und nach des alten Königs Tode bekam er das Reich.

Then he brought his father and mother, and they lived in
joy with their son, and after the old king's death he got the
kingdom.

Der Dreschflegel vom Himmel

The Flail from Heaven

1.1 Es zog einmal ein Bauer mit einem Paar Ochsen zum Pflügen aus.

Once a farmer went out plowing with a pair of oxen.

1.2 Als er auf den Acker kam, da fingen den beiden Tieren die Hörner an zu wachsen, wuchsen fort, und als er nach Hause wollte, waren sie so groß, daß er nicht mit zum Thor hinein konnte.

When he came to the field, the two animals' horns began to grow, grew away, and when he wanted to go home they were so big that he could not go in the gate with them.

1.3 Zu gutem Glück kam gerade ein Metzger daher, dem überließ er sie, und schlossen sie den Handel dergestalt, daß er sollte dem Metzger ein Maß Rübsamen bringen, der wollte ihm dann für jedes Korn einen brabanter Thaler aufzählen.

Fortunately a butcher came along just then, to whom he gave them, and they made a bargain in such a way that he was to bring the butcher a measure of turnip-seed, who would then give him a Brabant thaler for each grain.

Das heiß ich gut verkauft! 1.4
That was a good sale!

Der Bauer ging nun heim, und trug das Maß 1.5
Rübsamen auf dem Rücken herbei; unterwegs verlor
er aber aus dem Sack ein Körnchen.
So the farmer went home, carrying the measure of
rapeseed on his back, but on the way he lost a grain from
his sack.

Der Metzger bezahlte ihn wie gehandelt war richtig 1.6
aus;
The butcher paid him as he had done;

hätte der Bauer das Korn nicht verloren, 1.7
if the farmer had not lost the grain,

so hätte er einen brabanter Thaler mehr gehabt. 1.8
he would have had one thaler more.

Indessen, wie er wieder des Weges zurückkam, war 1.9
aus dem Korn ein Baum gewachsen, der reichte bis an
den Himmel.
Meanwhile, as he came back along the road, the grain had
grown into a tree that reached up to the sky.

Da dachte der Bauer: 1.10
Then the farmer thought,

»Weil die Gelegenheit da ist, mußt du doch sehen, 1.11
was die Engel da droben machen, und ihnen einmal
unter die Augen gucken.«
"Since the opportunity is there, you must see what the
angels are doing up there, and have a look under their
eyes."

1.12 Also stieg er hinauf und sah, daß die Engel oben Hafer droschen und schaute das mit an; wie er so, schaute, merkte er; daß der Baum, worauf er stand, anfing, zu wackeln, guckte hinunter und sah, daß ihn eben einer umhauen wollte.

So he climbed up and saw that the angels were threshing oats above, and looked at them, and as he looked he noticed that the tree on which he was standing was beginning to shake, so he looked down and saw that one of them was about to knock him down.

1.13 »Wenn du da herabstürztest, das wäre ein böses Ding.«

"If you were to fall down there, it would be a bad thing."

1.14 dachte er, und in der Not wußte er sich nicht besser zu helfen, als daß er die Spreu vom Hafer nahm, die haufenweise da lag und daraus einen Strick drehte;

thought he, and in his distress he knew no better way than to take the chaff from the oats, which lay there in heaps, and twist a rope from it;

1.15 auch griff er nach einer Hacke und einem Dreschflegel, die da herum im Himmel lagen, und ließ sich an dem Seil herunter.

he also seized a hoe and a flail, which were lying about in the sky, and let himself down by the rope.

Er kam aber unten auf der Erde gerade in ein tiefes,   1.16
tiefes Loch, und da war es ein rechtes Glück, daß
er die Hacke hatte, denn er hackte sich damit
eine Treppe, stieg in die Höhe und brachte den
Dreschflegel zum Wahrzeichen mit, sodaß niemand
an seiner Erzählung mehr zweifeln konnte.

But he came to a deep, deep hole on the ground below, and
it was quite fortunate that he had the hoe, for he hoed a
stairway with it, climbed up into the air, and brought the
flail with him as a symbol, so that no one could doubt his
story any longer.

De beiden Künigeskinner
The Two Kings Children

1.1 Et was mol en Künig west, de hadde en kleinen Jungen kregen, in den sin Teiken (Zeichen) hadde stahn, he sull von einen Hirsch ümmebracht weren, wenn he sestein Johr alt wäre.

There was once a king in the west who had a little boy with a sign in his pocket that he would be killed by a stag when he was a year old.

1.2 Ase he nu so wit anewassen was,

When he was so young,

1.3 do gingen de Jägers mol mit ünne up de Jagd.

the hunters went hunting with him.

1.4 In den Holte, do kümmt de Künigssohn bie de anneren denne (von den anderen weg), up einmol süht he do ein grooten Hirsch, den wull he scheiten, he kunn en awerst nig dreppen;

The king's son came into the wood with the others (away from the others), at one point he saw a large stag there, which he wanted to kill, but he couldn't kill it;

203

up't lest is de Hirsch so lange für ünne herut laupen, 1.5
bis gans ut den Holte, do steiht do up einmol so ein
grot lank Mann stad des Hirsches, de segd:

at last the stag came out for him until he was completely
out of the wood, and at one point there was a large, long
man standing next to the stag, who said:

»Nu, dat is gut, dat ik dik hewe; 1.6

"Well, it's good that I've got it;

ik hewe schon sess paar gleserne Schlitschau hinner 1.7
die kaput jaget un hewe dik nig kriegen könnt.«

I've already hunted a few smooth slithers behind the
broken one and couldn't get it."

Do nümmet he ün mit sik un schlippet em dur ein 1.8
grot Water, bis für en grot Künigsschlott, da mut he
mit an'n Disk un eten wat.

Then he took one with him and slipped it through a large
body of water until he reached a large royal chimney,
where he went to the disk and ate something.

Ase se tosammen wat geeten hed, segd de Künig: 1.9

When they had finished their meal together, the king said:

»Ik hewe drei Döchter, bie der ölesten mußt du en 1.10
Nacht waken, von des Obends niegen Uhr bis Morgen
sesse, un ik kumme jedesmal wenn de Klocke schlätt,
sülwens un rope, un wenn du mie dann kine Antwort
givst, so werst du morgen ümmebracht, wenn du
awerst mie immer Antwort givst, so salst du se tor
Frugge hewen.«

"I have three daughters, you have to spend the night with
the eldest one, from the end of the night until morning,
and I'll come every time the bell tolls, every night and
every day, and if you don't give me an answer then, you'll
be taken away tomorrow, but if you always give me an
answer, you'll have to keep her for a long time."

1.11 Ase do die jungen Lude up de Schlopkammer kämen, do stund der en stelneren Christoffel, do segd de Künigsdochter to emme:

When the young lads came to the bedroom, there stood a stony Christoffel, and the king's daughter said to him:

1.12 »Um niegen Uhr kummet min Teite (Vater), alle Stunne bis et dreie schlätt, wenn he froget, so giwet gi em Antwort statt des Künigssuhns.«

"My father comes at noon, every hour until three o'clock, if he asks, I'll give him an answer instead of the king's son."

1.13 Do nickede de steinerne Christoffel mit den Koppe gans schwinne un dann jümmer lanksamer, bis he toleste wier stille stand.

Then the stone Christoffel nodded his head and then nodded longer and longer until he stood still again.

1.14 Den anneren Morgen, da segd de Künig to emme:

The next morning, the king said to him:

1.15 »Du hest dine Sacken gut macket, awerst mine Dochter kann ik nig hergiewen, du möstest dann en Nacht bie de tweiden Dochter wacken, dann will ik mie mal drup bedenken, ob du mine ölleste Dochter tor Frugge hewen kannst, awerst ik kumme olle Stunne sülwenst, un wenn ik die rope, so antworte mie, un wenn ik die rope un du antwortest nig, so soll fleiten din Blaud für mie.«

"You have made your sack well, but I can't bring my daughter here, you want to spend a night with your two daughters, then I want to think about whether you can keep my oldest daughter in bed, but if I get all the hours, then answer me, and if I don't answer and you don't answer, then let your blue hair fly for me."

Un do gengen de beiden up de Schlopkammer, do
stand do noch en gröteren steineren Christoffel, dato
seg de Künigsdochter:

1.16

And then the two of them went up to the bedroom, where
a larger, stonier Christoffel stood, and the king's daughter
said:

»Wenn mine Teite frögt, so antworte du.«

1.17

"If my side answers, you answer."

Do nickede de grote, steinerne Christoffel, wier
mit dem Koppe gans schwinne un dann jümmer
lanksamer, bis he toleste wier stille stand.

1.18

Then the large, stony Christoffel nodded, his head became
very weak and then became longer and longer until he
stood still.

Un de Künigssuhn legte sik up dem Dörsüll
(Thürschwelle),

1.19

And the king's son lay down on the doorstep,

legte de Hand unner den Kopp un schläp inne.

1.20

put his hand under his head and fell asleep.

Den anneren Morgen seh de Künig to ünne:

1.21

The next morning the king looked at him:

»Du hast dine Sacken twaren gut macket, awerst
mine Dochter kann ik nig hergiewen, du möstest süs
bie der jungesten Künigsdochter en Nacht wacken,
dann will ik mie bedenken, ob du mine tweide
Dochter tor Frugge hewen kannst;

1.22

"You have made your sack well, but I can't bring my
daughter here, you want to spend the night with the
youngest king's daughter, then I will consider whether
you can bring my two daughters to bed;

1.23 awerst ik kumme olle Stunne sülwenst un wenn ik die rope, so antworte mie, un wenn ik die rope un du antwortest nig, so soll fleiten din Bland für mie.«

but if I come to you all night, and if I answer the rope, then answer me, and if I answer the rope and you don't answer, then your land shall fly for me."

1.24 Do gingen se wier tohope (zusammen) up ehre Schlopkammer, do was do noch en viel grötern un viel längern Christoffel, ase bie de twei ersten.

Then they went back to their bedroom, where there was a much bigger and much longer Christoffel than the first two.

1.25 Dato segte de Künigsdochter: »Wenn min Teite röpet,

Then the king's daughter said: "If my side is calling,

1.26 so antworte du.«

you answer."

1.27 do nickede de grote lange steinerne Christöffel wohl ene halwe Stunne mit den Koppe, bis de Kopp tolest wier stille stand.

The big long stone spoon nodded its head for half an hour until the head was still.

1.28 Un de Künigssuhn legte sik up de Dörsüll un schläp inne.

And the king's son lay down in the village and fell asleep.

1.29 Den annern Morgen, do segd de Künig:

The next morning, the king said:

»Du hast twaren gut wacket, awerst ik kann die nau mine Dochter nig giewen, ik hewe so en groten Wall, wenn du mie den von hüte morgen sesse bis obends sesse afhoggest, so will ik mie drup bedenken.« 1.30

"You've done well, but I can't give them to my daughter, I have such a big wall, if you take it down from the top of the morning to the top of the night, I'll think about it."

Do dehe (that, d. i. gab) he ünne en gleserne Exe, en glesernen Kiel un en gleserne Holthacke midde. 1.31

Then he dehe (that, i.e. gave) himself a smooth exe, a smooth keel and a smooth wooden heel.

Wie he in dat Holt kummen is, do hoggete he einmal to, do was de Exe entwei; 1.32

As he came into the harbor, he went up once, then the eel was empty;

do nam he den Kiel un schlett einmal mit de Holthacke daruppe, 1.33

then he named the keel and dragged it once with the wooden hoe,

do is et so kurt un so klein ase Grutt (Sand). 1.34

then it was so short and so small as grass (sand).

Do was he so bedröwet un glövte nu möste he sterwen, 1.35

Then he was so bedridden and thought he would die,

un he geit sitten un grient (weint). Asset nu Middag is, 1.36

and he went to sit and cry. Asset nu Middag is,

do segd de Künig: 1.37

do segd de Künig:

1.38 »Eine von juck Mäken mott ünne wat to etten bringen.«

"Eine von juck Mäken mott ünne wat to etten bring."

1.39 »Nee.« segged de beiden öllesten,

"No." said the two oldest,

1.40 »wie willt ün nicks bringen, wo he dat leste bie wacket het, de kann ün auck wat bringen.«

"how can you bring something when you're the youngest."

1.41 Do mutt de jungeste weg un bringen ünne wat to etten.

So the youngest ones had to leave and bring us something to eat.

1.42 Ase in den Walle kummet, dö fragt se ün wie et ünne ginge?

When he came into the hall, she asked him how he was doing?

1.43 »O.« sehe he, »et ginge ün gans schlechte.«

"Oh." he says, "it's going really badly."

1.44 Do sehe se, he sull herkommen un etten eest en bitken.

Then he sees that he should come here and ask a question.

1.45 »Ene.« sehe he,

"No." he saw,

1.46 »dat künne he nig, he möste jo doch sterwen, etten wull he nig mehr.«

"he couldn't, he would have to die, he didn't want to anymore."

Do gav se ünne so viel gute Woore, he möchte et doch   1.47
versöken;
She gave him so many good words, he wanted to
make up for it;

do kümmt he un ett wat. Ase he wat getten hett, do   1.48
sehe se:
so he came and did something. When he said something,
she said:

»Ik will die eest en bitken lusen,   1.49
"I want to give you a little more,

dann werst du annerst to Sinnen.«   1.50
then you'll come to your senses again."

Do se ün luset, do werd he so möhe un schlöppet in,   1.51
un do nümmet se ehren Doock un binnet en Knupp
do in, un schlätt ün dreimal up de Eere un segd:
When she laughed, he became so happy and slipped in, and
then she took her dock and put a knob in it, and slapped it
three times on the egg and said:

»Arweggers, herut!«   1.52
"Arweggers, here!"

Do wuren gliek so viele Eerdmännekens herfur   1.53
kummen un hadden froget, wat de Künigsdochter
befelde.
So many earthlings came here and asked what the king's
daughter was doing.

Do seh se: 1.54
Then they saw:

1.55 »In Tied von drei Stunnen mutt de grote Wall
afhoggen un olle dat Holt in Hüpen settet sien.«
"Within three hours, the great wall must go down and all
the wood must be put in its place."

1.56 Do gingen de Eerdmännekens herum un boen ehre
ganse Verwanschap up, dat se ehnen an de Arweit
helpen sullen.
Then the earthmen went around and told their whole
administration that they should help them with their
work.

1.57 Do fingen se gliek an, un ase de drei Stunne ümme
würen, do is olles to Enne (zu Ende) west, un do
keimen se wier to der Künigsdochter un sehent ehr.
Then they began again, and as the three hours passed,
everything came to an end, and then they returned to the
king's daughter and saw her.

1.58 Do nümmet se wier ehren witten Doock un segd:
»Arweggers,
Then she takes her white coat and says: "Arweggers,

1.59 nah Hus!« Do siet se olle wier wege west.
near the house!" Then she all went west again.

1.60 Do de Künigssuhn upwacket, so werd he so frau, do
segd se:
When the king's wife woke up, she said:

1.61 »Wenn et nu sesse schloen het, so kumme nah Hus.«
"If it's closed now, come to the house."

1.62 Dat het he auck bevolget, un do frägt de Künig:
He did the same, and then the king asked:

1.63 »Hest du den Wall aawe (ab)?«
"Have you taken down the wall?"

»Jo.« segd de Künigssuhn. Ase se do an een Diske   1.64
sittet,
"Yes." said the king's son. As she sits there at a desk,

do seh de Künig: 1.65
the king sees:

»Ik kann di nau mine Dochter nie tor Frugge giewen,   1.66
"I can't give you my daughter anything to look at,

he möste eest nau wat umme se dohen.«   1.67
he just has to do something about her."

Do frägt he, wat dat denn sien sulle.   1.68
Then he asked what it was.

»Ik hewe so en grot Dieck.« seh de Künig,   1.69
"I've got such a big box." the king said,

»do most du den annern Morgen hünne un most   1.70
en utschloen, dat he so blank is ase en Spegel, un et
müttet von ollerhand Fiske dorinne sien.«
"you'll have to make the other morning thinner and
smoother, so that it's as bare as a spear, and there should be
fish in there from all sides."

Den anneren Morgen do gav ünne de Künig ene   1.71
gleserne Schute (Schüppe) un segd:
The next morning, the king gave him a smooth bowl and
said:

»Umme sess Uhr mot de Dieck ferrig sien.«   1.72
"The deck has to be ready at six o'clock."

1.73 **Do geit he weg, ase he bi den Dieck kummet, do stecket he mit de Schute in de Muhe (Moor, Sumpf), do brack se af, do stecket he mit de Hacken in de Muhe, un et was wier kaput.**

Then he goes away, as he arrives at the dock, he sticks the barge in the mire (bog, swamp), it breaks, he sticks his heels in the mire, and it was broken again.

1.74 **Do werd he gans bedröwet.**

Then he was completely covered.

1.75 **Den Middag brachte de jüngeste Dochter ünne wat to etten do frägt se,**

In the middle of the day,

1.76 **wo et ünne ginge?**

the youngest daughter brought him something to eat and asked where he was?

1.77 **Do seh de Künigssuhn, et ginge ünne gans schlechte, he sull sienen Kopp wohl mißen mutten:**

Then the king's son saw that it was going very badly, he must have had a bad headache:

1.78 **»Dat Geschirr is mie wir klein gohen.«**

"The dishes are small."

1.79 **»O.« seh se, »he sull kummen un etten eest wat,**

"Oh." she said, "he should come and eat something,

1.80 **dann werst du anneren Sinnes.«**

then you'll be of a different mind."

1.81 **»Nee.« segte he, »etten kunn he nig,**

"No." he said, "he can't eat anything,

1.82 **he wer gar to bedröwet.«**

he's too tired."

Do givt se ünne viel gude Woore, bis he kummet un ett watt.
1.83

Then she gave him a lot of good words until he came and got some water.

Do luset se ünn wier, un he schloppet in;
1.84

Then she smiles at him again and he slips in;

se nümmet von niggen en Doock,
1.85

she takes a dock from the other side,

schlett en Knupp do inne un kloppet mit den Knuppe dreimol up de Eere un segt:
1.86

drags a knob in there and knocks the knob three times on the egg and says:

»Arweggers, herut!«
1.87

"Arweggers, here!"

Do kummt gliek so viele Eerdmännekens un froget olle wat ehr Begeren wür.
1.88

Then so many people from the earth come and ask everyone what their companion was.

In Tied von drei Stunne mosten se den Dieck gans utschloen hewen, un he möste so blank sien, dann man sik inne speigelen künne, un von ollerhand Fiske mosten dorinne sien.
1.89

Within three hours, they had to have the dock completely closed, and it had to be so clean that you could spit in it, and there had to be fish in it from all sides.

Do gingen de Eerdmännekens hünn un boen ehre Verwanschap up, dat se ünnen helpen sullen;
1.90

Then the earthmen went up and offered their help;

un et is auck in zwei Stunnen ferrig west.
1.91

and it was over in two hours.

1.92 **Do kummet se wier un seged: »Wie hät dohen,**
Then they came back and said: "As they have done,

1.93 **so us befolen is.«**
so have we."

1.94 **Do nümmet de Künigsdochter den Doock un schlett wier dreimol up de Eere un segd:**
Then the King's Daughter takes the dock and slides up to the egg three times and says:

1.95 **»Arweggers, to Hus!« Do siet se olle wier weg.**
"Arweggers, to the house!" Then she is all gone again.

1.96 **Ase do de Künigssuhn upwacket, do is de Dieck ferrig.**
When the king's son wakes up, the dock is ready.

1.97 **Do geit de Künigsdochter auck weg un segd, wenn et sesse wär, dann sull he nah Hus kummen.**
Then the king's daughter goes away and says that if it's all right, he should come to the house.

1.98 **Ase he do nah Hus kummet, do frägt de Künig:**
When he arrives at the house, the king asks:

1.99 **»Hes du den Dieck ferrig?«**
"Have you finished the dieck?"

1.100 **»Jo.« seh de Künigssuhn. Dat wür schöne.**
"Yes." said the king's son. That would be nice.

1.101 **Do se do wier to Diske sittet, do seh de Künig:**
As she was sitting at the desk, the king saw:

»Du hast den Dieck twaren ferrig, awerst ik kann di 1.102
mine Dochter noch nie giewen, du most eest nau eins
dohen.«

"You've got the blanket ready, but I've never been able to
give it to my daughter, you've just got one."

»Wat is dat denn?« frögte de Künigssuhn. 1.103

"What's that then?" asked the king's son.

He hedde so en grot Berg, do würen lauter 1.104
Dorenbuske anne, de mosten alle afhoggen weren un
bowen up moste he en grot Schlott buggen, dat moste
so wacker sien, ase't nu en Menske denken kunne,
un olle Ingedömse, de in den Schlott gehorden, de
mosten der olle inne sien.

He had such a big mountain, there were all sorts of bushes
on it, they all had to be hauled up and he had to build a big
chimney, which had to be so sturdy that a man could now
think of it, and all the ingenuity that went into the chimney
had to be in there.

Do he nu den anneren Morgen up steit, 1.105

When he got up the next morning,

do gav ünne de Künig en glesernen Exen un en 1.106
glesernen Boren mie:

the king gave him a glass excrement and a glass bear:

et mott awerst um sess Uhr ferrig sien. 1.107

it had to be ready by six o'clock.

Do he an den eersten Dorenbuske mit de Exen 1.108
anhogget, do ging se so kurt un so klein, dat de
Stücker rund um ünne herfloen, un de Boren künn he
auck nig brücken.

When he arrived at the first door bus with the exes, they
were so short and so small that the pieces flew all around
him, and he couldn't even bridge them.

1.109 **Do war he gans bedröwet un toffte (wartcte) up sine Leiwestc,**
Then he was all dressed up and waited for his vest,

1.110 **op de nie keime un ünn ut de Naut hülpe.**
which never came off and helped him out of the water.

1.111 **Ase't do Middag is, do kummet se un bringet wat to etten;**
When it was midday, she came and brought something to eat;

1.112 **do geit he ehr in de Möte (entgegen) un verteilt ehr olles un ett wat,**
then he went to meet her and handed her everything and something,

1.113 **un lett sik von ehr lusen un schlöppet in.**
and let himself be lured by her and slipped in.

1.114 **Do nümmet se wier den Knupp un schlett domit up de Eere un segd:**
Then she takes the knob and drags it up to the egg and says:

1.115 **»Arweggers, herut!«**
"Arweggers, here!"

1.116 **Do kummet wier so viel Eerdmännekens un fraget, wat ehr Begeren wür?**
Then we come to so many earthlings and ask what their companion was?

1.117 **Do seh se:**
Then they saw:

»In Tied von drei Stunnen müttet ju den gansen
Busk afhoggen, un bowen uppe den Berge do mott en
Schlott stohen, dat mot so wacker sien, ase't nu ener
denken kann, un olle Ingedömse muttet do inne sien.
"In three hours, you have to walk the whole bus, and there
has to be a chimney up the mountain, which has to be as
sturdy as you can imagine, and all of the ingenuity has to be
there.

1.118

Do ginge se hünne un boen ehre Verwanschap up, dat
se helpen sullen, un ase te Tied umme was, do was
alles ferrig.
Then they went up and offered their help, and when the
time came, everything was ready.

1.119

Do kümmet se to der Künigsdochter un segget dat,
Then she went to the King's Daughter and told her,

1.120

un de Künigsdochter nümmet den Döoock und
schlett dreimal domit up de Eere uni segd:
and the King's Daughter took the dock and dragged it up to
the egg three times and said:

1.121

»Arweggers to Hus!« Do siet se gliek olle wier weg
west.
"Arweggers to Hus!" Then she is all gone again.

1.122

Dö nu de Künigssuhn upwecket, un olles soh, do was
he so frau ase en Vugel in der Lust.
Then the king's son woke up, and everything was like a bird
in the sky.

1.123

Do et do sesse schloen hadde, do gingen se tohaupe
nah Hus.
When it was time to sit down, they went home.

1.124

Do segd de Künig: »Is dat Schlott auck ferrig'?«
Then the king said: "Is the pot still ready?"

1.125

1.126 »Jo.« seh de Königssuhn. Ase do to Diske sittet,
"Yes," said the king's son. As they were sitting at the desk,

1.127 do segd de Künig:
the king said:

1.128 »Mine jungeste Dochter kann ik nie giewen, befur detwei öllesten frigget het.«
"I can never tell my youngest daughter why she has eaten the most."

1.129 Do wor de Künigssuhn un de Künigsdöchter gans bedröwet,
Then the king's son and the king's daughters were very distressed,

1.130 un de Künigssuhn wuste sik gar nig to bergen (helfen).
and the king's son didn't know how to help.

1.131 Do kummet he mol bie Nachte to der Künigsdochter un löppet dermit furt.
So he came to the king's daughter in the night and took her for a walk.

1.132 Ase do en bitken wegsiet,
When a little bit went away,

1.133 do ticket sik de Dochter mol umme un süht ehren Vader hinner sik.
the daughter turned around and saw her father behind her.

1.134 »O.« seh se, »wo sull wie dat macken?
"Oh." she says, "where are we going to do that?

1.135 Min Vader is hinner us un will us ummeholen;
My father is behind us and wants to pick us up;

ik will die grade to'n Dörenbusk macken un mie 1.136
tor Rose un ik will mie ümmer midden in den Busk
waarn (schützen).«
I want to take her to the village bus and I want to keep her
in the middle of the bus."

Ase do de Vader an de Stelle kummet, 1.137
When the father comes to the place,

do steit do en Dörenbusk un ene Rose do anne; 1.138
there's a door and a rose standing there;

do will he de Rose afbrecken, do kummet de Dören 1.139
un stecket ün in de Finger, dat he wier nah Hus gehen
mut.
he wants to break the rose, then the door comes and sticks
his finger in, so that he has to go back home.

Do fragt sine Frugge, worumme he se nig hädde 1.140
middebrocht.
Then his wife asks him why he hadn't brought her home.

Do seh he, he wür der balt bie west, awerst he hedde 1.141
se uppen mol ut den Gesichte verloren, un do hädde
do en Dörenbusk un ene Rose stohen.
Then he saw that he was the old one in the west, but he had
lost sight of her once again, and there was a bush and a
rose.

Do seh de Königin: 1.142
Then the queen saw:

»Heddest du ment (nur) de Rose afbrocken, 1.143
"If you had (only) broken the rose,

de Busk hedde sullen wohl kummen.« 1.144
the busk should have come."

1.145 **Do geit he wier weg un will de Rose herholen.**
So he goes away again and wants to fetch the rose.

1.146 **Unnerdes waren awerst de beiden schon wiet öwer Feld, un de Künig löppet der hinnerher.**
However, the two of them were already far across the field, and the king followed.

1.147 **Do kicket sik de Dochter wier umme un süht ehren Vader kummen;**
Then the daughter kicks around again and sees her father coming;

1.148 **do seh se: »O, wo sull wie et nu macken?**
then she says: "Oh, where should I do it now?

1.149 **Ik will die grade tor Kerke macken un mie tom Pastoer;**
I just want to do it at the church and to the pastor;

1.150 **do will ik up de Kanzel stohn un priedigen.«**
then I want to stand up in the pulpit and pray."

1.151 **Ase do de Künig an de Stelle kummet, do steiht do ene Kerke, un up de Kanzel is en Pastoer un priediget;**
When the king came to the place, there stood a candle, and there was a pastor and a priest in the pulpit;

1.152 **do hort he de Priedig to un geit wier nah Hus.**
then he stopped the pulpit and went back to the house.

1.153 **Do fragt de Küniginne, worumme he se nig middebrocht hedde, da segd he:**
Then the queen asks him why he didn't have it in the middle, and he says:

»Nee, ik hewe se so lange nachlaupen, un as ik glovte, ik wer der hold bie, do steit do en Kerke un up de Kanzel en Pastoer, de priedigte.« 1.154

"No, I've been lapping it up for so long, and when I realized I was the one who was holding it, there's a candle there and a pastor in the pulpit."

»Du häddest sullen ment den Pastoer bringen.« seh de Fru, 1.155

"You should have brought the pastry." the woman said,

»de Kerke hädde sullen wohl kummen; 1.156

"the candle should have come;

dat ik die auck (wenn ich dich auch) schicke, dat kann nig mer helpen, ik mut sülwenst hünne gohen.« 1.157

I can't help but send it, I have to go to the church first."

Ase se do ene Miele wege is un de beiden von fern süht, 1.158

When she is a mile away and sees the two of them from afar,

do kicket sik de Künigsdochter umme un süht ehre Moder kummen un segd: 1.159

the king's daughter kicks around and sees her mother coming and says:

»Nu sie wie unglücksk, nu kummet miene Moder sülwenst! 1.160

"How unfortunate, now my mother is coming to me!

Ik will die grade tom Dieck macken un mie tom Fisk.« 1.161

I just want to take her to the corner and me to the window."

1.162 Do de Moder up de Stelle kummet, do is do en grot Dieck, un in de Midde sprank en Fisk herumme un kickete mit den Kopp ut den Water un was gans lustig.

When the moderator came to the spot, there was a big hole, and in the middle a fisk jumped around and kicked its head out of the water and was really funny.

1.163 Do wüll se geren den Fisk krigen,

She wanted to catch the fisk,

1.164 awerst se kunn ünn gar nig fangen.

but she couldn't catch anything.

1.165 Do werd se gans böse un drinket den gansen Dieck ut, dat se den Fisk kriegen will, awerst do werd se so üwel, dat se sick spiggen mott un spigget den gansen Dieck wier ut.

Then she got really angry and drank the whole thing to get the fish, but then she got so mad that she had to spit and spit the whole thing out again.

1.166 Do seh se:

Then she saw:

1.167 »Ik sehe do wohl, dat et olle nig mer helpen kann.«

"I can see that there's nothing else that can help."

1.168 Sei mogten nu wier to ehr kummen.

They now had to come back to her.

1.169 Do göhet se dann auck wier hünne,

Then they went back to her,

1.170 un de Küniginne givt der Dochter drei Walnütte un segd:

and the queen gave her daughter three walnuts and said:

»Do kannst du die mit helpen, wenn du in dine högste 1.171
Naud bist.«

"You can help them when you're in your highest
neighborhood."

Un do gingen de jungen Lüde wier tohaupe weg. 1.172

And then the young girls went away again.

De se do wohl kein Stunne gohen hadden, do kummet 1.173
se an dat Schlott, wovon de Kunigssuhn was, un
dobie was en Dorp.

Since they probably didn't have an hour to go, they came to
the chimney where the Kunigssuhn was, and there was a
village.

Ase se do anne keimen, do segd de Künigssuhn: 1.174

When they arrived there, the king's wife said:

»Blief hie, mine Leiweste, ik will eest up dat Schlott 1.175
gohen, un dann will ik mit den Wagen un Bedeinten
kummen un will die afholen.«

"Stay here, my wife, I want to go to the castle first, and then
I want to come with the wagons and the beds and pick them
up."

Ase he do up dat Schlott kummet do werd se olle so 1.176
frau,

When he came up to the castle,

dat se den Künigssuhn nu wier hett; 1.177

she was all so mad that she now had the king's son;

do vertellt he, he hedde ene Brut un de wür jetzt in 1.178
den Dorpe, se wullen mit den Wagen hintrecken un
se holen.

then he said that he had a brood and they were now in the
village, they wanted to go back with the wagon and fetch
her.

1.179 **Do spannt se auck gliek an, un viele Bedeinten setten sich up den Wagen.**

So they hitched up the wagon and many people sat on it.

1.180 **Ase do de Künigssuhn instiegen wull, do gav ün sine Moder en Kus, do hadde he alles vergeten, wat schehen was un auck wat he dohen will.**

As the king's son was about to get in, his mother gave him a kiss, he had forgotten everything that had happened and what he wanted to do.

1.181 **Do befal de Moder, se sullen wier utspannen, un do gingen se olle wier in't Hus.**

Then the moderator told them to relax again, and they all went back to the house.

1.182 **Dat Mäken awerst sitt im Dorpe un luert un luert un meint, he sull se afholen, et kummet awerst keiner.**

The girl, however, sits in the village and lurks and lurks and thinks he should pick her up, but no one comes.

1.183 **Do vermaiet (vermietet) sik de Känigsdochter in de Muhle, de hoerde bie dat Schlott, do moste se olle Nohmiddage bie den Watter sitten un Stunze schüren (Gefäße reinigen).**

Then the king's daughter hires herself out to the mill, she listens at the chimney, she has to sit in the mudflats and clean the pots.

1.184 **Do kummet de Küniginne mol von den Schlotte gegohen un gohet an den Water spazeiern, un seihet dat wackere Mäken do sitten, do segd se:**

Then the queen came back from the chimney and went to the water, and when she saw the brave girl sitting there, she said:

»Wat is dat für en wacker Mäken! Wat gefüllt mie dat gut!« 1.185

"What a brave girl! How good it fills me up!"

Do kicket se et olle an, awerst, keen Menske hadde et kand. 1.186

Then they all kicked at it, but no one knew it.

Do geit wohl ene lange Tied vorbie, dat dat Mäken eerlick un getrugge bie den Müller deint. 1.187

It must have been a long time since the girl had been seen and carried away by the miller.

Unnerdes hadde de Küniginne ene Frugge für ehren Suhn socht, de is gans feren ut der Weld west. 1.188

In addition, the queen had made a mug for her son, which was far away from the field.

Ase do de Brut ankümmet, 1.189

As soon as the brood arrived,

do söllt se gliek tohaupe giewen weren. 1.190

they were to be given a new home.

Et laupet so viele Lüde tosamen de dat olle seihen willt, do segd dot Mäken to den Müller, he mögte ehr doch auck Verlöb giewen. 1.191

There are so many people together who want to see it all, so the girl says to the miller that he should give her a dowry.

Do seh de Müller: »Goh menten hünne.« 1.192

Then the miller sees: "Go on, stay here."

1.193 Ase't do weg will, do macket et ene van den drei Walnütten up, do legt do so en wacker Kleid inne, dat trecket et an un gienk domie in de Kerke gigen den Altor stohen.

When he wants to leave, one of the three huts opens, puts on a brave dress, puts it on and goes to stand in the candle at the altar.

1.194 Up enmol kummt de Brut un de Brüme (Bräutigam), un settet sik für den Altor, un ase de Pastoer se do insegnen wull, do kicket sik de Brut van der Halwe (seitwärts), un süht et do stohen, do steit se wier up und segd, se wull sik nie giewen loten, bis se auck so en wacker Kleid hädde, ase de Dame.

Once the bride and groom came and sat down for the altar, and when the pastor wanted to inaugurate them, the bride kicked herself from the neck (sideways) and saw them standing there, then she stood up again and said that she never wanted to let herself go until she had a dress as bold as the lady.

1.195 Do gingen se wier nah Hus un läten de Dame froen, ob se dat Kleid wohl verkofte.

So they went back to the house and asked the lady if she was wearing the dress.

1.196 Nee, verkaupen dau seit nig, awerst verdeinen, dät mögte wohl sien.

No, she didn't want to sell it, but she did want to wear it.

1.197 Do fragten se ehr, wat se denn dohen sullen.

Then they asked her what they wanted to do.

1.198 Do segd se, wenn se van Nachte fur dat Dohr van den Künigssuhn schlapen döffte, dann wull se et wohl dohen.

Then she said that if she could sleep at night for the king's son, then she would probably do it.

227

Do seget se jo, dat sul se menten dohen. 1.199
Then she said that she wanted to do it.

Do muttet de Bedeinten den Künigssuhn en 1.200
Schlopdrunk ingiewen, un do legt se sik up den
Süll un günselt (winselt) de heile Nacht, se hädde
den Wall für ün afhoggen loten, se hädde de Dieck
für ün utschloen, se hädde dat Schlott für ün bugget,
se hädde ünne ton Dörenbusk macket dann wier
tor Kerke ün tolest tom Dieck, un he hädde se so
geschwinne vergete.
Then the bedridden woman would give the king a drink,
and then she would lie down on the coffin and whimper
the good night, she would let the wall down for us, She had
the wall closed for us, she had the vent opened for us, she
had made a new sound of the doorway, and then she had a
candle to the wall, and he had forgotten her so well.

De Küigssuhn hadde nicks davon hört, de Bedeinten 1.201
awerst würen upwacket un hadden tolustert un
hadden nie wust, wat et sull bedüen.
The chickens hadn't heard a word about it, but the children
had woken up and were shaking their heads, never
knowing what it meant.

Den anneren Morgen, ase se upstöen würen, do trock 1.202
de Brut dat Kleid an, un fort mit den Brumen nah der
Kerke.
The next morning, when they woke up, the brood dried
their clothes and left with the flowers near the candle.

Unnerdes macket dat wackere Mäken de tweide 1.203
Walnutt up, un do is nau en schöner Kleid inne dat
thütet wier an un geit domie in de Kerke gigen den
Altor stohen;
Then the brave girl opens the two walnuts, and there is a
beautiful dress inside, which we put on and go to the candle
at the altar;

228

1.204 do geit et dann ewen wie dat vürgemol.
then it goes as it did before.

1.205 Un dat Mäken liegt wier en Nacht für den Süll, de nah
des Kühnigssuhns Stobe geit, un de Bedeinten füllt
ün wier en Schlopdrunk ingiewen;
And the miller lies like a night for the swell, which
goes near the bold shoe, and the bedding fills us like a
Schlopdrunk ingiewen;

1.206 de Bedeinte kummet awerst un giewet ünne wat to
wacken,
the bedding comes first and gives ünne something to
wacken,

1.207 domie legt he sik to Bedde;
domie legt he sik sik to Bedde;

1.208 un de Müllersmaged fur den Dörsüll günselt wier so
viel un segd,
and the Müllersmaged für den Dörsüll günselt wier so viel
und segd,

1.209 wat se dohen hädde.
was sie dohen hädde.

1.210 Dat hört olle de Künigssuhn un werd gans bedröwet,
Everyone hears the king's voice and becomes very sad,

1.211 un et söllt ünne olle wier bie wat vergangen was.
and it seems to everyone that something has happened.

1.212 Do will he nah ehr gohen,
Then he wanted to go to her,

1.213 awerst sine Moder hadde de Dör toschlotten.
but his mother was still sleeping in the village.

Den annern Morgen awerst ging he gliek to siner
Leiwesten un vertellte ehr olles, wie et mit ünne
togangen wür, un se mögte ünne doch nig beuse sin
dat he se so lange vergeiten hädde.

1.214

The next morning, however, he went straight to his vest
and told her everything that had happened to her, and she
couldn't be sorry that he had missed her for so long.

Do macket de Künigsdochter de dridde Walnutt up,

1.215

Then the King's Daughter opens the third walnut,

do is nu en viel wackerer Kleid inne:

1.216

and there is now a much braver dress inside:

dat trecket sie an un fört mit ehrem Brümen nah de
Kerke, un do keimen so viele Kinner, de geiwen ünne
Blomen un hellen ünne bunte Bänner fur de Föte, un
se leiten sik insegnen un hellen ene lustige Hochtied;

1.217

she steps on it and takes her breasts to the candle, and so
many children sprout, they grow thin flowers and light
thin colorful ribbons for the feet, and they lead themselves
in and light up a cheerful high tide;

awerst de falske Moder un Brut mosten weg.

1.218

but the false fashion and brood must go away.

Un we dat lest vertellt het, den is de Mund noch
warm.

1.219

And for those who have read this, their mouths are still
warm.

230

Vom klugen Schneiderlein

From the Clever Little Tailor

1.1   Es war einmal eine Prinzessin gewaltig stolz;
Once upon a time a princess was very proud;

1.2   kam ein Freier, so gab sie ihm etwas zu raten auf, und
wenn er's nicht erraten konnte, so ward er mit Spott
fortgeschickt.
when a suitor came, she gave him a riddle to guess, and if
he could not guess it, he was sent away with ridicule.

1.3   Sie ließ auch bekannt machen, wer ihr Rätsel löste,
sollte sich mit ihr vermählen, und möchte kommen,
wer da wollte.
She also let it be known that whoever solved her
riddle would marry her, and whoever wanted to come
would do so.

1.4   Endlich fanden auch drei Schneider zusammen,
davon meinten die zwei ältesten, sie hätten so
manchen feinen Stich gethan und hätten's getroffen,
da könnt's ihnen nicht fehlen, sie müßten's auch hier
treffen;
At last three tailors came together, of whom the two eldest
said that they had made many a fine stitch and had hit it, so
they could not fail to hit it here;

der dritte war ein kleiner unnützer Springinsfeld, der 1.5
nicht einmal sein Handwerk verstand, aber meinte,
er müßte dabei Glück haben, denn woher sollt's ihm
sonst kommen.

the third was a little useless jumper, who did not even
understand his trade, but thought he must be lucky, for
where else would it come to him.

Da sprachen die zwei anderen zu ihm: »Bleib nur zu 1.6
Hause,

Then the two others said to him, "Just stay at home,

du wirst mit deinem bißchen Verstande nicht weit 1.7
kommen!«

you won't get far with your little brains!"

Das Schneiderlein ließ sich aber nicht irre machen 1.8
und sagte, er hätte einmal seinen Kopf darauf gesetzt
und wollte sich schon helfen, und ging dahin, als
wäre die ganze Welt sein.

But the little tailor would not be deceived, and said that he
had once set his head on it, and wanted to help himself, and
went along as if the whole world were his.

Da meldeten sich alle drei bei der Prinzessin und 2.1
sagten, sie sollte ihnen ihre Rätsel vorlegend:

Then all three came to the princess and said that she should
present them with their riddles:

es wären die rechten Leute angekommen, die hätten 2.2
einen feinen Verstand, daß man ihn wohl in eine
Nadel fädeln könnte.

the right people had arrived, they had a fine mind that
could be threaded into a needle.

Da sprach die Prinzessin, 2.3

Then said the princess,

2.4 »Ich habe zweierlei Haare auf dem Kopfe,
"I have two kinds of hair on my head,

2.5 von was Farben sind sie?«
of what colors are they?"

2.6 »Wenn's weiter nichts ist.« sagte der erste,
"If it is nothing else." said the first,

2.7 »es wird schwarz und weiß sein, wie Tuch, das man
Kümmel und Salz nennt.«
"it will be black and white, like cloth called caraway and
salt."

2.8 Die Prinzessin sprach: »Falsch geraten.«
The princess said, "Wrong guess."

2.9 antwortete der zweite, da sagte der zweite:
answered the second, and then the second said,

2.10 »Ist's nicht schwarz und weiß, so ist's braun und rot,
wie meines Herrn Vaters Bratenrock.«
"If it is not black and white, it will be brown and red, like
my father's roast skirt."

2.11 »Falsch geraten.« sagte die Prinzessin, antwortete der
dritte,
"Wrong guess." said the princess, and the third replied,

2.12 »dem seh ich's an, der weiß es sicherlich.«
"I can tell by looking at him, he certainly knows."

2.13 Da trat das Schneiderlein keck hervor und sprach:
Then the little tailor came forward boldly and said,

»Die Prinzessin hat ein silbernes und ein goldenes
Haar auf dem Kopfe,

2.14

"The princess has silver and gold hair on her head,

und das sind die zweierlei Farben.«

2.15

and those are the two different colors."

Wie die Prinzessin das hörte, ward sie blaß und
wäre vor Schrecken beinahe hingefallen, denn
das Schneiderlein hatte es getroffen, und sie hatte
fest geglaubt, das würde kein Mensch auf der Welt
herausbringen.

2.16

When the princess heard this, she turned pale and almost
fell down from fright, for the little tailor had hit it, and she
had firmly believed that no one in the world would be able
to tell.

Als ihr das Herz wieder kam, sprach sie,

2.17

When her heart came back to her, she said,

»Damit hast du noch nicht gewonnen, du mußt noch
eins thun:

2.18

"You have not yet won, you must do one more thing:

unten im Stalle liegt ein Bär,

2.19

there is a bear down in the stable,

bei dem sollst du die Nacht zubringen;

2.20

and you shall spend the night with him;

wenn ich dann morgen aufstehe und du bist noch
lebendig,

2.21

if I get up tomorrow and you are still alive,

so sollst du mich heiraten.«

2.22

you shall marry me."

2.23 Sie dachte aber, damit wollte sie das Schneiderlein los werden, denn der Bär hatte noch keinen Menschen lebendig gelassen, der ihm unter die Tatzen gekommen war.

But she thought this was to get rid of the little tailor, for the bear had not yet left a single person alive who had come under his paws.

2.24 Das Schneiderlein ließ sich nicht abschrecken,

The little tailor was not deterred,

2.25 war ganz vergnügt und sprach:

was quite amused and said:

2.26 »Frisch gewagt ist halb gewonnen.«

"A new dare is half the battle."

3.1 Als nun der Abend kam,

When evening came,

3.2 ward mein Schneiderlein hinunter zum Bären gebracht.

my little tailor was taken down to the bear.

3.3 Der Bär wollte auch gleich auf den kleinen Kerl los und ihm mit seiner Tatze einen guten Willkommen geben.

The bear immediately wanted to attack the little fellow and give him a good welcome with his paw.

3.4 »Sachte, sachte.« sprach das kleine Schneiderlein,

"Easy, easy." said the little tailor,

3.5 »ich will dich schon zur Ruhe bringen.«

"I want to put you to rest."

Da holte es ganz gemächlich, als hätte es keine
Sorgen, welsche Nüsse aus der Tasche, biß sie auf
und aß die Kerne.

3.6

Then, as if he had no worries, he took some nuts out of his
pocket, bit them open and ate the kernels.

Wie der Bär das sah,

3.7

When the bear saw this,

kriegte er Lust und wollte auch Nüsse haben.

3.8

he got an appetite and wanted some nuts too.

Das Schneiderlein griff in die Tasche und reichte ihm
eine Hand voll; es waren aber keine Nüsse, sondern
Wackersteine.

3.9

The little tailor reached into his pocket and handed him a
handful, but they were not nuts, but wobbly stones.

Der Bär steckte sie ins Maul, konnte aber nichts
aufbringen, er mochte beißen wie er wollte.

3.10

The bear put them in his mouth, but couldn't find anything,
he could bite as much as he wanted.

»Ei.« dachte er, »was bist du für ein dummer Klotz!

3.11

"Oh." he thought, "what a stupid clod you are!

Kannst nicht einmal die Nüsse aufbeißen.«

3.12

You can't even bite open the nuts."

und sprach zum Schneiderlein: »Mein, beiß mir die
Nüsse auf.«

3.13

and said to the little tailor, "My, bite open my nuts."

»Da siehst du, was du für ein Kerl bist.«

3.14

"There you see what a fellow you are."

sprach das Schneiderlein,

3.15

said the little tailor,

236

3.16 »hast so ein großes Maul und kannst die kleine Nuß nicht aufbeißen.«

"you have such a big mouth and can't bite open the little nut."

3.17 Da nahm es die Steine, war hurtig, steckte dafür eine Nuß in den Mund und knack, war sie entzwei.

So he took the stones, was quick, put a nut in his mouth and cracked it in two.

3.18 »Ich muß das Ding noch einmal probieren.« sprach der Bär,

"I must try the thing again." said the bear,

3.19 »wenn ich's so ansehe, ich mein, ich müßt's, auch können.«

"when I look at it like that, I think I ought to be able to do it too."

3.20 Da gab ihm das Schneiderlein abermals Wackersteine,

Then the little tailor again gave him some wobbly stones,

3.21 und der Bär arbeitete und biß aus allen Leibeskräften hinein.

and the bear worked and bit into them with all his might.

3.22 Aber du glaubst auch nicht, daß er sie aufgebracht hat.

But you won't believe that he brought them up.

3.23 Wie das vorbei war,

When that was over,

3.24 holte das Schneiderlein eine Violine unter dem Rock hervor und spielte sich ein Stückchen darauf.

the little tailor took a violin from under his skirt and played a little piece on it.

Als der Bär die Musik vernahm, konnte er es nicht   3.25
lassen und fing an zu tanzen, und als er ein Weilchen
getanzt hatte, gefiel ihm das Ding so wohl, daß er
zum Schneiderlein sprach,
When the bear heard the music, he could not help it, and
began to dance, and when he had danced a little while, he
liked the thing so well that he said to the little tailor,

»Hör, ist das Geigen schwer?«   3.26
"Listen, is it difficult to play the violin?"

»Kinderleicht;   3.27
"Very easy;

siehst du, mit der Linken leg ich die Finger auf und   3.28
mit der Rechten streich ich mit dem Bogen drauf los,
da geht's lustig, hopsasa, vivallalera!«
you see, I put my fingers on it with my left hand, and with
my right I stroke it with the bow, and it's fun, hopsasa,
vivallalera!"

»So geigen.« sprach der Bär,   3.29
"Fiddle like that." said the bear,

»das möcht ich auch verstehen, damit ich tanzen   3.30
könnte, so oft ich Lust hätte.
"I'd like to understand that too, so that I could dance as
often as I felt like it.

Was meinst du dazu? Willst du mir Unterricht darin   3.31
geben?«
What do you think? Will you give me lessons?"

»Von Herzen gern.« sagte das Schneiderlein,   3.32
"With all my heart." said the little tailor,

»wenn du Geschick dazu hast.   3.33
"if you have the skill.

3.34 Aber weis einmal deine Tatzen her, die sind gewaltig lang, ich muß dir die Nägel ein wenig abschneiden.«

But show me your paws, they are very long, I must cut off your nails a little."

3.35 Da ward ein Schraubstock herbeigeholt und der Bär legte seine Tatzen darauf, das Schneiderlein aber schraubte sie fest und sprach,

Then a vice was fetched and the bear put his paws on it, but the little tailor screwed them tight and said,

3.36 »Nun warten bis ich mit der Schere komme.«

"Now wait till I come with the scissors."

3.37 ließ den Bären brummen, soviel er wollte, legte sich in die Ecke auf ein Bund Stroh und schlief ein.

He let the bear grumble as much as he liked, lay down in the corner on a bundle of straw and fell asleep.

4.1 Die Prinzessin, als sie am Abend den Bären so gewaltig brummen hörte, glaubte nicht anders, als er brummte vor Freuden und hätte dem Schneider den Garaus gemacht.

The princess, when she heard the bear growling so violently in the evening, could not help thinking that he was growling with joy and would have killed the tailor.

4.2 Am Morgen stand sie ganz unbesorgt und vergnügt auf;

In the morning she got up quite unconcerned and happy;

4.3 wie sie aber nach dem Stall guckt,

but when she looked into the stable,

4.4 so steht das Schneiderlein ganz munter davor und ist gesund wie ein Fisch im Wasser.

the little tailor was standing in front of it as lively and healthy as a fish in water.

Da konnte sie nun kein Wort mehr dagegen sagen, 4.5
weil sie's öffentlich versprochen hatte, und der König
ließ einen Wagen kommen, darin mußte sie mit dem
Schneiderlein zur Kirche fahren und sollte sie da
vermählt werden.
Now she could not say a word against it, because she had
promised it publicly, and the King sent for a carriage, in
which she was to go to church with the little tailor, and
there she was to be married.

Wie sie eingestiegen waren, gingen die beiden 4.6
anderen Schneider, die ein falsches Herz hatten
und ihm sein Glück nicht gönnten, in den Stall und
schraubten den Bären los.
As soon as they had got in, the two other tailors, who had a
false heart and did not begrudge him his happiness, went
into the stable and unscrewed the bear.

Der Bär, in voller Wut, rannte hinter dem Wagen her. 4.7
The bear, in a rage, ran after the cart.

Die Prinzessin hörte ihn schnauben und brummen; 4.8
The princess heard him snorting and growling;

es ward ihr angst und sie rief: »Ach, 4.9
she was frightened and called out: "Oh,

der Bär ist hinter uns und will dich holen.« 4.10
the bear is behind us and wants to get you."

Das Schneiderlein war fix, stellte sich auf den Kopf, 4.11
stellte die Beine zum Fenster hinaus und rief,
The little tailor was quick, stood on his head, put his legs
out of the window and called out,

»Siehst du den Schraubstock? Wenn du nicht gehst, 4.12
"Do you see the vice? If you don't go,

4.13 so sollst du wieder hinein.« Wie der Bär das sah,
you shall go back in." When the bear saw this,

4.14 drehte er um und lief fort.
he turned around and ran away.

4.15 Mein Schneiderlein fuhr da ruhig in die Kirche und die Prinzessin ward ihm an die Hand getraut und lebte er mit ihr vergnügt wie eine Heidelerche.
My little tailor went quietly into the church, and the princess was married to him, and he lived with her as happily as a woodlark.

4.16 Wer's nicht glaubt, bezahlt einen Thaler.
If you don't believe it, pay a thaler.

Die Klare Sonne bringt's an den Tag

The Clear Sun Brings it to Light

1.1 Ein Schneidergesell reiste in der Welt auf sein Handwerk herum und konnte er einmal keine Arbeit finden und war die Armut bei ihm so groß,

A journeyman tailor was traveling the world at his trade,

1.2 daß er keinen Heller Zehrgeld hatte.

and once he could not find work and his poverty was so great that he had not a penny to his name.

1.3 In der Zeit begegnete ihm auf dem Wege ein Jude, und da dachte er, der hätte viel Geld bei sich und stieß Gott aus seinem Herzen, ging auf ihn los und sprach,

At that time he met a Jew on the road, and he thought he had a lot of money with him, so he pushed God out of his heart and went up to him and said,

1.4 »Gieb mir dein Geld oder ich schlage dich tot.«

"Give me your money or I'll kill you."

1.5 Da sagte der Jude: »Schenkt mir doch das Leben,

Then the Jew said: "Give me your life,

Geld hab ich keins und nicht mehr als acht Heller.«   1.6

I have no money and no more than eight pence."

Der Schneider aber sprach,   1.7

But the tailor said,

»Du hast doch Geld und das soll auch heraus.«   1.8

"You do have money and that's what I want."

brauchte Gewalt und schlug ihn so lange, bis er nahe   1.9
am Tode war.

He used force and beat him until he was close to death.

Und wie der Jude nun sterben wollte, sprach er das   1.10
letzte Wort:

And as the Jew was about to die, he said the last word:

»Die klare Sonne wird es an den Tag bringen!«   1.11

"The clear sun will bring it to light!"

und starb damit.   1.12

and died.

Der Schneidergesell griff ihm in die Tasche und   1.13
suchte nach Geld, er fand aber nicht mehr als die acht
Heller, wie der Jude gesagt hatte.

The journeyman tailor reached into his pocket and
searched for money, but found no more than the eight
pence the Jew had said he had.

Da packte er ihn auf,   1.14

So he picked him up,

trug ihn hinter einen Busch und zog weiter auf sein   1.15
Handwerk.

carried him behind a bush and set off on his journey.

244

1.16 Wie er nun lange Zeit gereist war, kam er in eine Stadt bei einem Meister in Arbeit, der hatte eine schöne Tochter, in die verliebte er sich und heiratete sie und lebte in einer guten vergnügten Ehe.

After he had traveled for a long time, he came to a town where he worked for a master craftsman who had a beautiful daughter, with whom he fell in love and married her and lived in a happy marriage.

2.1 Über lang, als sie schon zwei Kinder hatten, starben Schwiegervater und Schwiegermutter, und die jungen Leute hatten den Haushalt allein.

Long after they had two children, their father-in-law and mother-in-law died, leaving the young people to run the household alone.

2.2 Eines Morgens, wie der Mann auf dem Tische vor dem Fenster saß, brachte ihm die Frau den Kaffee, und als er ihn in die Unterschale ausgegossen hatte und eben trinken wollte, da schien die Sonne darauf und der Wiederschein blinkte oben an der Wand so hin und her und machte Kringel daran.

One morning, as the husband was sitting on the table in front of the window, the wife brought him his coffee, and when he had poured it into the saucer and was about to drink it, the sun shone on it and the reflection flashed back and forth on the wall above, making curls on it.

2.3 Da sah der Schneider hinauf und sprach: »Ja,

Then the tailor looked up and said, "Yes,

2.4 die will's gern an den Tag bringen und kann's nicht!«

she wants to bring it to light and can't!"

2.5 Die Frau sprach: »Ei, lieber Mann, was ist denn das?

The woman said, "Oh, dear man, what is that?

Was meinst du damit?« Er antwortete: 2.6
What do you mean by that?" He replied:

»Das darf ich dir nicht sagen.« Sie aber sprach, 2.7
"I'm not allowed to tell you that." But she said,

»Wenn du mich lieb hast, müßt du mir's sagen.« 2.8
"If you love me, you must tell me."

und gab ihm die allerbesten Worte, 2.9
and gave him the very best words that no man should know
it again,

es sollt's kein Mensch wieder erfahren und ließ ihm 2.10
keine Ruhe.
and left him no peace.

Da erzählte er, vor langen Jahren, wie er auf der 2.11
Wanderschaft ganz abgerissen und ohne Geld
gewesen, habe er einen Juden erschlagen, und
der Jude habe in der letzten Todesangst die Worte
gesprochen,
Then he told him that long years ago, when he was
wandering about, and had been quite torn up and without
money, he had slain a Jew, and that the Jew, in his last
agony, had spoken the words,

»Die klare Sonne wird's an den Tag bringen!« 2.12
"The clear sun will bring it to light!"

Nun hätt's die Sonne eben gern an den Tag bringen 2.13
wollen und hätt' an der Wand geblinkt und Kringel
gemacht,
Now the sun would have liked to bring it to light and would
have flashed on the wall and made squiggles,

sie hätt's aber nicht gekonnt. 2.14
but she couldn't do it.

2.15 Danach bat er sie noch besonders, sie dürfte es
niemand sagen, sonst käm er um sein Leben, das
versprach sie auch.

Afterwards he asked her especially not to tell anyone,
otherwise he would lose his life, and she promised.

2.16 Als er sich aber zur Arbeit gesetzt hatte, ging sie zu
ihrer Gevatterin und vertraute ihr die Geschichte, sie
dürfe sie aber keinem Menschen wieder sagen; ehe
aber drei Tage vergingen, wußte es die ganze Stadt;
und der Schneider kam vor das Gericht und ward
gerichtet.

But when he had set to work, she went to her godmother
and confided the story to her, but she must not tell it to
any one again; but before three days had passed, the whole
town knew it, and the tailor came before the court and was
judged.

2.17 Da brachte es doch die klare Sonne an den Tag.

Then the clear sun brought it to light.

Das blaue Licht

The Blue Light

1.1 Es war einmal ein Soldat, der hatte dem König lange Jahre treu gedient;

Once upon a time there was a soldier who had served the king faithfully for many years;

1.2 als aber der Krieg zu Ende war und der Soldat, der vielen Wunden wegen, die er empfangen hatte, nicht weiter dienen konnte, sprach der König zu ihm,

but when the war was over and the soldier could no longer serve because of the many wounds he had received, the king said to him,

1.3 »Du kannst heim gehen, ich brauche dich nicht mehr;

"You can go home, I don't need you any more;

1.4 Geld bekommst du weiter nicht, denn Lohn erhält nur der, welcher mir Dienste dafür leistet.«

you won't get any more money, for wages are only given to those who render me service in return."

1.5 Da wußte der Soldat nicht, womit er sein Leben fristen sollte;

Then the soldier did not know what to do for a living;

249

ging voll Sorgen fort und ging den ganzen Tag, bis er abends in einen Wald kam.   1.6

he went away full of worries and walked all day until he came to a forest in the evening.

Als die Finsternis einbrach, sah er ein Licht, dem näherte er sich und kam zu einem Hause, darin wohnte eine Hexe.   1.7

As darkness fell, he saw a light, which he approached and came to a house where a witch lived.

»Gieb mir doch ein Nachtlager und ein wenig Essen und Trinken.«   1.8

"Give me a place to stay for the night and some food and drink."

sprach er zu ihr, »ich verschmachte sonst!«   1.9

he said to her, "otherwise I'll starve to death!"

»Oho.« antwortete sie,   1.10

"Oh no." she replied,

»wer giebt einem verlaufenem Soldaten etwas?   1.11

"who gives anything to a lost soldier?

Doch will ich barmherzig sein und dich aufnehmen, wenn du thust, was ich verlange.«   1.12

But I will be merciful and take you in if you do as I ask."

»Was verlangst du?« fragte der Soldat.   1.13

"What do you ask?" asked the soldier.

»Daß du mir morgen meinen Garten umgräbst.«   1.14

"That you dig up my garden tomorrow."

1.15 Der Soldat willigte ein und arbeitete den folgenden Tag aus allen Kräften, konnte aber vor Abend nicht fertig werden.
The soldier agreed, and worked the next day with all his might, but could not finish before evening.

1.16 »Ich sehe wohl.« sprach die Hexe,
"I see." said the witch,

1.17 »daß du heute noch nicht weiter kannst;
"that you cannot go on today;

1.18 ich will dich noch ein Nacht behalten,
I will keep you one more night,

1.19 dafür sollst du mir morgen ein Fuder Holz spalten und klein machen.«
but tomorrow you shall split a load of wood for me and make it small."

1.20 Der Soldat brauchte dazu den ganzen Tag, und abends machte ihm die Hexe den Vorschlag, noch eine Nacht zu bleiben.
It took the soldier all day, and in the evening the witch suggested that he stay another night.

1.21 »Du sollst mir Morgen nur eine geringe Arbeit thun, hinter meinem Hause ist ein alter wasserleerer Brunnen, in den ist mir mein Licht gefallen, es brennt blau und verlischt nicht, das sollst du mir wieder herauf holen.«
"Tomorrow you shall only do a little work for me, there is an old well behind my house that is empty of water, my light has fallen into it, it burns blue and does not go out, you shall bring it up for me again."

Den anderen Tag führte ihn die Alte zu dem Brunnen und ließ ihn in einem Korbe hinab.   1.22

The next day the old woman took him to the well and let him down in a basket.

Er fand das blaue Licht und machte ein Zeichen,   1.23

He found the blue light,

daß sie ihn wieder hinaufziehen sollte.   1.24

and made a sign that she should draw him up again.

Sie zog ihn auch in die Höhe, als er aber dem Rand nahe war, reichte sie die Hand hinab und wollte ihm das blaue Licht abnehmen.   1.25

She also pulled him up, but when he was near the edge, she reached down and wanted to take the blue light from him.

»Nein!« sagte er und merkte ihre bösen Gedanken,   1.26

"No!" he said, realizing her evil thoughts,

»das Licht gebe ich dir nicht eher, als bis ich mit beiden Füßen auf dem Erdboden stehe.«   1.27

"I won't give you the light until I have both feet on the ground."

Da geriet die Hexe in Wut ließ ihn wieder hinab in den Brunnen fallen und ging fort.   1.28

Then the witch became furious, dropped him back down into the well and went away.

Der arme Soldat fiel ohne Schaden zu nehmen auf den feuchten Boden, und das blaue Licht brannte fort, aber was konnte ihm das helfen?   2.1

The poor soldier fell to the damp ground without harm, and the blue light burned away, but what good could it do him?

2.2 Er sah wohl, daß er dem Tode nicht entgehen würde.

He could see that he would not escape death.

2.3 Er saß eine Weile ganz traurig, da griff er zufällig in seine Tasche und fand seine Tabakspfeife, die noch halb gestopft war.

He sat for a while, quite sad, when he happened to reach into his pocket and found his tobacco pipe, which was still half filled.

2.4 »Das soll mein letztes Vergnügen sein.«

"This shall be my last pleasure."

2.5 dachte er, zog sie heraus, zündete sie an dem blauen Licht an und fing an zu rauchen.

he thought, pulled it out, lit it by the blue light and began to smoke.

2.6 Als der Dampf in der Höhle umhergezogen war,

As the vapor drifted around the cave,

2.7 stand auf einmal ein kleines schwarzes Männchen vor ihm und fragte:

a little black man suddenly stood in front of him and asked:

2.8 »Herr, was befiehlst du?«

"Lord, what do you command?"

2.9 »Was habe ich dir zu befehlen?«

"What do I have to tell you?"

2.10 erwiderte der Soldat ganz verwundert. »Ich muß alles thun«

replied the soldier in astonishment. "I must do"

2.11 sagte das Männchen, »was du verlangst.«

said the little man, "everything you ask."

»Gut.« sprach der Soldat, 2.12
"Well." said the soldier,

»so hilf mir zuerst aus dem Brunnen.« 2.13
"first help me out of the well."

Das Männchen nahm ihn bei der Hand und führte 2.14
ihn durch einen unterirdischen Gang,
The little man took him by the hand and led him through
an underground passage,

vergaß aber nicht das blaue Licht mitzunehmen. 2.15
but did not forget to take the blue light with him.

Es zeigte ihm unterwegs die Schätze, welche die Hexe 2.16
zusammengebracht und da versteckt hatte, und der
Soldat nahm so viel Gold als er tragen konnte.
On the way, he showed him the treasures that the witch
had brought together and hidden there, and the soldier
took as much gold as he could carry.

Als er oben war, sprach er zu dem Männchen: 2.17
When he reached the top, he said to the little man:

»Nun geh hin, binde die alte Hexe und führe sie vor 2.18
das Gericht.«
"Now go and bind the old witch and bring her before the
court."

Nicht lange, so kam sie auf einem wilden Kater 2.19
mit furchtbarem Geschrei schnell wie der Wind
vorbeigeritten, und es dauerte abermals nicht lange,
so war das Männchen zurück.
It was not long before she came riding past on a wild cat,
screaming like the wind, and it was not long before the
little man was back.

2.20 »Es ist alles ausgerichtet.« sprach es,
"Everything is ready." he said,

2.21 »und die Hexe hängt schon am Galgen. – Herr,
"and the witch is already hanging on the gallows. – Sir,

2.22 was befiehlst du weiter?« fragte der Kleine.
what do you say?" asked the little man.

2.23 »In dem Augenblick nichts.« antwortete der Soldat,
"Nothing at present." replied the soldier,

2.24 »du kannst nach Hause gehen;
"you can go home;

2.25 sei nur gleich bei der Hand, wenn ich dich rufe.«
just be ready when I call you."

2.26 »Es ist nichts nötig.« sprach das Männchen,
"Nothing is necessary." said the little man,

2.27 »als daß du deine Pfeife an dem blauen Licht
anzündest,
"but that you light your pipe by the blue light,

2.28 dann stehe ich gleich vor dir.«
and I will stand before you at once."

2.29 Darauf verschwand es vor seinen Augen.
Then he disappeared before his eyes.

3.1 Der Soldat kehrte in die Stadt zurück, aus der er
gekommen war.
The soldier returned to the town from which he had come.

Er ging in den besten Gasthof und ließ sich schöne
Kleider machen, dann befahl er dem Wirt, ihm ein
Zimmer so prächtig als möglich einzurichten.

3.2

He went to the best inn and had beautiful clothes made for
himself, then ordered the innkeeper to furnish a room for
him as splendidly as possible.

Als es fertig war und der Soldat es bezogen hatte, rief
er das schwarze Männchen und sprach:

3.3

When it was ready and the soldier had moved in, he called
the little black man and said,

»Ich habe dem König treu gedient, er aber hat mich
fortgeschickt und mich hungern lassen, dafür will
ich jetzt Rache nehmen.«

3.4

"I have served the king faithfully, but he has sent me away
and left me hungry, for which I will now take revenge."

»Was soll ich thun.« fragte der Kleine.

3.5

"What shall I do." asked the little boy.

»Spät abends, wenn die Königstochter im Bett liegt,
so bring sie schlafend hierher, sie soll Mägdedienste
bei mir thun.«

3.6

"Late in the evening, when the king's daughter is in bed,
bring her here asleep and let her do maid's work for me."

Das Männchen sprach:

3.7

The little man said,

»Für mich ist das ein leichtes, für dich aber ein
gefährliches Ding, wenn das herauskommt, wird
es dir schlimm ergehen.«

3.8

"That is an easy thing for me, but a dangerous thing for you;
if it comes out, it will be bad for you."

3.9 Als es zwölf geschlagen hatte, sprang die Thür auf, und das Männchen trug die Königstochter herein.

When it had struck twelve, the door burst open, and the little man carried the king's daughter in.

3.10 »Aha, bist du da?« rief der Soldat,

"Aha, are you there?" cried the soldier,

3.11 »frisch an die Arbeit! Geh, hole den Besen und kehr die Stube.«

"get to work! Go, get the broom and sweep the room."

3.12 Als sie fertig war, hieß er sie zu seinem Sessel kommen, streckte ihr die Füße entgegen und sprach,

When she had finished, he ordered her to come to his chair, stretched out his feet to her and said,

3.13 »Zieh mir die Stiefel aus.«

"Take off my boots."

3.14 warf sie ihr dann ins Gesicht und sie mußte sie aufheben,

He then threw them in her face and she had to pick them up,

3.15 reinigen und glänzend machen.

clean them and make them shiny.

3.16 Sie that aber alles, was er ihr befahl, ohne Widerstreben, stumm und mit halbgeschlossenen Augen.

But she did everything he told her to do without resistance, silently and with half-closed eyes.

Bei dem ersten Hahnschrei trug sie das Männchen
wieder in das königliche Schloß und in ihr Bett
zurück.

3.17

At the first cry of the cock she carried the little man back to
the royal palace and to her bed.

Am anderen Morgen, als die Königstochter
aufgestanden war, ging sie zu ihrem Vater und
erzählte ihm, sie hätte einen wunderlichen Traum
gehabt:

4.1

The next morning, when the King's daughter had risen, she
went to her father and told him that she had had a strange
dream:

»Ich ward durch die Straßen mit Blitzesschnelle
fortgetragen und in das Zimmer eines Soldaten
gebracht, dem mußte ich als Magd dienen und
aufwarten und alle gemeine Arbeit thun, die Stube
kehren und die Stiefel putzen.

4.2

"I was carried away through the streets at lightning speed
and brought to a soldier's room, where I had to serve as a
maid and wait on him and do all the common work, sweep
the room and clean his boots.

Es war nur ein Traum, und doch bin ich so müde, als
wenn ich wirklich alles gethan hätte.«

4.3

It was only a dream, and yet I am as tired as if I had really
done it all."

»Der Traum könnte wahr gewesen sein.« sprach der
König,

4.4

"The dream might have been true." said the King,

4.5 »ich will dir einen Rat geben, stecke deine Tasche voll Erbsen und mache ein kleines Loch in die Tasche, wirst du wieder abgeholt, so fallen sie heraus und lassen die Spur auf der Straße.«

"I will give you a piece of advice, put your pocket full of peas and make a little hole in it, and when you are picked up again they will fall out and leave the trail on the road."

4.6 Als der König so sprach,

As the king spoke,

4.7 stand das Männchen unsichtbar dabei und hörte alles mit an.

the little man stood invisibly by and listened to everything.

4.8 Nachts, als es die schlafende Königstochter wieder durch die Straßen trug, fielen zwar einzelne Erbsen aus der Tasche, aber sie konnten keine Spur machen, denn das listige Männchen hatte vorher in allen Straßen Erbsen verstreut.

At night, when he carried the sleeping king's daughter through the streets again, a few peas fell out of the bag, but they could not leave a trace, for the cunning little man had previously scattered peas in all the streets.

4.9 Die Königstochter aber mußte wieder bis zum Hahnenschrei Mägdedienste thun.

The king's daughter, however, had to do maid's work again until cockcrow.

5.1 Der König schickte am folgenden Morgen seine Leute aus, welche die Spur suchen sollten, aber es war vergeblich, denn in allen Straßen saßen die armen Kinder und lasen Erbsen auf und sagten,

The next morning the king sent out his people to search for the trail, but it was in vain, for the poor children were sitting in all the streets picking up peas and saying,

»Es hat heute nacht Erbsen geregnet.«   5.2

"It has rained peas tonight."

»Wir müssen etwas anderes aussinnen.« sprach der   5.3
König,

"We must think of something else." said the king,

»behalte deine Schuhe an, wenn du dich zu Bett legst,   5.4
und ehe du von dort zurückkehrst, verstecke einen
davon, ich will ihn schon finden.«

"keep your shoes on when you go to bed, and before you
return from there, hide one of them, I will find it."

Das schwarze Männchen vernahm den Anschlag,   5.5
und als der Soldat abends verlangte, er sollte die
Königstochter wieder herbeitragen, riet er es ihm ab
und sagte, gegen diese List wüßte es kein Mittel, und
wenn der Schuh bei ihm gefunden würde, so könnte
es ihm schlimm ergehen.

The little black man heard the plot, and when the soldier
demanded in the evening that he should carry the king's
daughter back to him, he dissuaded him, saying that he
knew no remedy for this trick, and that if the shoe were
found on him it might be a bad thing for him.

»Thue was ich dir sage.« erwiderte der Soldat,   5.6

"Do as I say." replied the soldier,

und die Königstochter mußte auch in der dritten   5.7
Nacht wie eine Magd arbeiten;

and on the third night the King's daughter had to work like
a maid;

sie versteckte aber, ehe sie zurückgetragen wurde,   5.8
einen Schuh unter das Bett.

but before she was carried back she hid a shoe under the
bed.

6.1 Am anderen Morgen ließ der König in der ganzen Stadt den Schuh seiner Tochter suchen;

The next morning the king had his daughter's shoe searched for throughout the town;

6.2 er ward bei dem Soldaten gefunden, und der Soldat selbst, der sich auf Bitten des Kleinen zum Thor hinaus gemacht hatte, ward bald eingeholt und ins Gefängnis geworfen.

it was found with the soldier, and the soldier himself, who had gone out to the gate at the little boy's request, was soon caught and thrown into prison.

6.3 Er hatte sein Bestes bei der Flucht vergessen, das blaue Licht und das Gold, und hatte nur noch einen Dukaten in der Tasche.

He had forgotten the best he had in his flight, the blue light and the gold, and had only one ducat left in his pocket.

6.4 Als er nun mit Ketten belastet an dem Fenster seines Gefängnisses stand, sah er einen seiner Kameraden vorbeigehen.

As he stood at the window of his prison, burdened with chains, he saw one of his comrades pass by.

6.5 Er klopfte an die Scheibe, und als er herbeikam, sagte er:

He knocked on the window, and when he came over, he said,

6.6 »Sei so gut und hol mir das kleine Bündelchen, das ich in dem Gasthause habe liegen lassen, ich gebe dir dafür einen Dukaten.«

"Be so good as to fetch me the little bundle I left at the inn, and I'll give you a ducat for it."

Der Kamerad lief hin und brachte ihm das Verlangte. 6.7
The comrade ran over and brought him what he had asked
for.

Sobald der Soldat wieder allein war, 6.8
As soon as the soldier was alone again,

steckte er seine Pfeife an und ließ das schwarze 6.9
Männchen kommen.
he lit his pipe and sent for the little black man.

»Sei ohne Furcht.« sprach es zu seinem Herrn, 6.10
"Be unafraid." he said to his master,

»geh hin wo sie dich hinführen und laß alles 6.11
geschehen,
"go where they lead you and let everything happen,

nimm nur das blaue Licht mit.« 6.12
just take the blue light with you."

Am anderen Tage ward Gericht über den Soldaten 6.13
gehalten, und obgleich er nichts Böses gethan hatte,
verurteilte ihn der Richter doch zum Tode.
The next day the soldier was tried, and although he had
done nothing wrong, the judge condemned him to death.

Als er nun hinausgeführt wurde, 6.14
When he was led out,

bat er den König um eine letzte Gnade. »Was für 6.15
eine?«
he asked the king for one last mercy. "What kind?"

fragte der König. 6.16
asked the king.

6.17 »Daß ich auf dem Wege noch eine Pfeife rauchen darf.«

"That I may smoke one more pipe on the way."

6.18 »Du kannst drei rauchen.« antwortete der König,

"You can smoke three." replied the king,

6.19 »aber glaube nicht, daß ich dir das Leben schenke.«

"but don't think I'm giving you life."

6.20 Da zog der Soldat seine Pfeife heraus und zündete sie an dem blauen Licht an, und wie ein paar Ringel vom Rauch aufgestiegen waren, so stand schon das Männchen da, hatte einen kleinen Knüppel in der Hand und sprach,

Then the soldier took out his pipe and lighted it by the blue light, and as a few ringlets of smoke rose up, the little man stood there with a small club in his hand, and said,

6.21 »Was befiehlt mein Herr?«

"What does my lord command?"

6.22 »Schlag mir da die falschen Richter und ihre Häscher zu Boden, und verschone auch den König nicht, der mich so schlecht behandelt hat.«

"Smite the false judges and their henchmen to the ground, and do not spare the king who has treated me so badly."

6.23 Da fuhr das Männchen wie der Blitz, zickzack, hin und her, und wen es mit seinem Knüppel nur anrührte, der fiel schon zu Boden und getraute sich nicht mehr zu regen.

Then the little man zigzagged back and forth like lightning, and whoever he touched with his club fell to the ground and dared not move.

Dem König ward angst, er legte sich auf das Bitten,   6.24
und um nur das Leben zu behalten, gab er dem
Soldaten das Reich und seine Tochter zur Frau.

The king was afraid, he gave in to the pleading, and to save
his life he gave the soldier the kingdom and his daughter to
wife.

Das eigensinnige Kind
The Stubborn Child

1.1 **Es war einmal ein Kind eigensinnig und that nicht, was seine Mutter haben wollte.**
Once upon a time a child was stubborn and did not do what his mother wanted.

1.2 **Darum hatte der liebe Gott kein Wohlgefallen an ihm und ließ es krank werden und kein Arzt konnte ihm helfen,**
Therefore the good God was not pleased with him and allowed him to fall ill and no doctor could help him,

1.3 **und in kurzem lag es auf dem Totenbettchen.**
and in a short time he lay on his deathbed.

Als es nun ins Grab versenkt und die Erde darüber 1.4
hingedeckt war, so kam auf einmal sein Ärmchen
wieder hervor und reicht in die Höhe, und wenn sie
es hineinlegten und frische Erde darüber thaten, so
half das nicht, und das Ärmchen kam immer wieder
heraus.

When she was lowered into the grave and the earth was
covered over her, suddenly her little arm came out again
and reached up, and when they put it in and put fresh earth
over it, it did not help, and the little arm came out again
and again.

Da mußte die Mutter selbst zum Grabe gehen und 1.5
mit der Rute auf's Ärmchen schlagen, und wie sie das
gethan hatte, zog es sich hinein, und das Kind hatte
nun erst Ruhe unter der Erde.

Then the mother had to go to the grave herself, and beat the
little arm with the rod, and as she had done so, it drew itself
in, and the child was now at rest under the earth.

Die drei Feldscherer

The Three Feldsher

1.1 Drei Feldscherer reisten in der Welt, die meinten, ihre Kunst ausgelernt zu haben und kamen in ein Wirtshaus, wo sie übernachten wollten.

Three feldshermen were traveling around the world who thought they had mastered their art and came to an inn where they wanted to spend the night.

1.2 Der Wirt fragte, wo sie her wären und hinaus wollten?

The innkeeper asked where they were from and where they were going?

1.3 »Wir ziehen auf unsere Kunst in der Welt herum.«

"We are traveling the world on our art."

1.4 »Zeigt mir doch einmal, was ihr könnt.« sagte der Wirt.

"Show me what you can do." said the innkeeper.

1.5 Da sprach der erste, er wolle seine Hand abschneiden und morgen früh wieder anheilen;

Then the first said he would cut off his hand and heal it again in the morning;

der zweite sprach, er sein Herz ausreißen und
morgen früh wieder anheilen;
the second said he would tear out his heart and heal it again
in the morning;

1.6

der dritte sprach, er wollte seine Augen ausstechen
und morgen früh, wieder einheilen.
the third said he would gouge out his eyes and heal them
again in the morning.

1.7

»Könnt ihr das.« sprach der Wirt,
"If you can do that." said the innkeeper,

1.8

»so habt ihr ausgelernt.«
"you have finished learning."

1.9

Sie hatten aber eine Salbe, was sie damit bestrichen,
das heilte zusammen und das Fläschchen, wo sie drin
war, trugen sie beständig bei sich.
But they had an ointment, which they spread on their eyes
and which healed them, and they always carried the small
bottle containing it with them.

1.10

Da schnitten sie Hand, Herz und Augen vom Leibe,
wie sie gesagt hatten, legten's zusammen auf einen
Teller und gabens dem Wirt;
Then they cut off their hands, hearts and eyes as they had
said, put them together on a plate and gave them to the
innkeeper;

1.11

der Wirt gab's einem Mädchen,
the innkeeper gave them to a girl,

1.12

das sollt's in den Schrank stellen und wohl aufheben.
who was to put them in the cupboard and keep them safe.

1.13

1.14 Das Mädchen aber hatte einen heimlichen Schatz,

But the girl had a secret treasure,

1.15 der war ein Soldat.

which was a soldier.

1.16 Wie nun der Wirt, die drei Feldscherer und alle Leute im Hause schliefen, kam der Soldat und wollte was zu essen haben.

While the landlord, the three feldsher and all the people in the house were asleep, the soldier came and wanted something to eat.

1.17 Da schloß das Mädchen den Schrank auf und holte ihm etwas, und über der großen Liebe vergaß es die Schrankthür zuzumachen, setzte sich zum Liebsten an den Tisch und sie schwatzten miteinander.

Then the girl opened the cupboard and got him something, and forgetting to shut the cupboard door because of her great love, she sat down at the table with her sweetheart and they talked together.

1.18 Wie es so vergnügt saß und an kein Unglück dachte, kam die Katze hereingeschlichen, fand den Schrank offen, nahm die Hand, das Herz und die Augen der drei Feldscherer und lief damit hinaus.

As he sat there happily, thinking of no misfortune, the cat crept in, found the cupboard open, took the hand, heart and eyes of the three soldiers and ran out with them.

1.19 Als nun der Soldat gegessen hatte und das Mädchen das Gerät aufheben und den Schrank zuschließen wollte, da sah es wohl, daß der Teller, den ihm der Wirt aufzuheben gegeben hatte, leer war.

When the soldier had eaten, and the girl was about to pick up the utensils and close the cupboard, she saw that the plate which the landlord had given her to pick up was empty.

Da sagte es erschrocken zu seinem Schatz,   1.20
Then she said to her treasure in horror,

»Ach was soll ich armes Mädchen anfangen! Die Hand   1.21
ist fort,
"Oh, what am I to do, poor girl! My hand is gone,

das Herz und die Augen; sind auch fort,   1.22
my heart and my eyes; they are gone too,

wie wird mir's morgen früh ergehen!«   1.23
how will I fare in the morning!"

»Sei still.« sprach der Soldat,   1.24
"Be quiet." said the soldier,

»ich will dir aus der Not helfen;   1.25
"I will help you out of your trouble;

es hängt ein Dieb draußen am Galgen,   1.26
there is a thief hanging on the gallows outside,

dem will ich die Hand abschneiden; welche Hand   1.27
war's denn?«
and I will cut off his hand; which hand was it?"

»Die rechte.«   1.28
"The right one."

Da gab ihm das Mädchen ein scharfes Messer und er   1.29
ging hin, schnitt dem armen Sünder die rechte Hand
ab und brachte sie herbei.
So the girl gave him a sharp knife and he went and cut off
the poor sinner's right hand and brought it back.

1.30 Darauf packte er die Katze und stach ihr die Augen aus;

Then he grabbed the cat and gouged out its eyes;

1.31 nun fehlte nur noch das Herz. »Habt ihr nicht geschlachtet?

now only the heart was missing. "Haven't you butchered it?

1.32 und liegt das Schweinefleisch nicht im Keller?«

And isn't the pork in the cellar?"

1.33 »Ja.« sagte das Mädchen. »Nun, das ist gut.«

"Yes." said the girl. "Well, that's good."

1.34 sagte der Soldat,

said the soldier,

1.35 ging hinunter und holte sich ein Schweineherz.

and went down and got himself a pig's heart.

1.36 Das Mädchen that alles zusammen auf einen Teller und stellte ihn in den Schrank, und als ihr Liebster darauf Abschied genommen hatte, legte er sich ruhig ins Bett.

The girl put it all together on a plate and put it in the cupboard, and when her beloved had taken his leave, he lay down quietly in bed.

2.1 Morgens, als die Feldscherer aufstanden, sagten sie dem Mädchen, es sollte ihnen den Teller holen, darauf Hand, Herz und Augen lägen.

In the morning, when the feldsher got up, they told the girl to fetch them the plate with the hand, heart and eyes on it.

Da brachte es ihn aus dem Schrank, und der erste hielt sich die Diebeshand an und bestrich sie mit seiner Salbe, alsbald war sie ihm angewachsen. 2.2
So she brought it out of the cupboard, and the first took the thief's hand and put his ointment on it, and it soon grew on him.

Der zweite nahm die Katzenaugen und heilte sie ein; 2.3
The second took the cat's eyes and cured them;

der dritte machte das Schweineherz fest. 2.4
the third fixed the pig's heart.

Der Wirt stand dabei, bewunderte ihre Kunst und sagte, dergleichen hätte er noch nicht gesehen; 2.5
The innkeeper stood by, admired their art and said he had never seen anything like it;

er wollte sie bei jedermann rühmen und empfehlen. 2.6
he wanted to praise and recommend them to everyone.

Darauf bezahlten sie ihre Zeche und reisten weiter. 2.7
Then they paid their bill and traveled on.

Wie sie so dahin gingen, so blieb der mit dem Schweineherzen gar nicht bei ihnen, sondern wo eine Ecke war, lief er hin und schnüffelte darin herum, wie Schweine thun. 3.1
As they walked along, the one with the pig's heart did not stay with them at all, but where there was a corner, he ran and sniffed around in it, as pigs do.

3.2 Die anderen wollten ihn an dem Rockschlippen zurückhalten, aber das half nichts, er riß sich los und lief hin, wo der dickste Unrat lag.

The others tried to hold him back by his coat-tails, but it was no use; he tore himself away and ran to where the thickest garbage lay.

3.3 Der zweite stellte sich auch wunderlich an, rieb die Augen und sagte zu dem anderen,

The second also acted strangely, rubbed his eyes and said to the other,

3.4 »Kamerad, was ist das?

"Comrade, what's that?

3.5 Das sind meine Augen nicht, ich sehe ja nichts, leite mich doch einer, daß ich nicht falle.«

It's not my eyes, I can't see anything, guide me so that I don't fall."

3.6 Da gingen sie mit Mühe fort bis zum Abend,

So they went on with difficulty till evening,

3.7 wo sie zu einer anderen Herberge kamen.

when they came to another inn.

3.8 Sie traten zusammen in die Wirtsstube, da saß in einer Ecke ein Herr vor dem Tisch und zählte Geld.

They entered the inn together, and there was a gentleman sitting in a corner before the table, counting money.

Der mit der Diebeshand ging um ihn herum, zuckte
ein paarmal mit dem Arm, endlich, wie der Herr sich
umwendete, griff er in den Haufen hinein und nahm
eine Handvoll Geld heraus.   3.9

The one with the thief's hand went round him, twitched
his arm a few times, and at last, as the gentleman turned
round, he reached into the heap and took out a handful of
money.

Der eine sah's und sprach: »Kamerad, was
machst du?   3.10

One of them saw it and said, "Comrade, what are you
doing?

Stehlen darfst du nicht, schäm dich!«   3.11

You mustn't steal, shame on you!"

»Ei.« sagte er, »was kann ich dafür!   3.12

"Well." he said, "what can I do about it!

Es zuckt mir in der Hand, ich muß zugreifen, ich mag
wollen oder nicht.«   3.13

It twitches in my hand, I must take it, I may want to or not."

Sie legten sich danach schlafen, und wie sie daliegen,
ist's so finster, daß man keine Hand vor Augen sehen
kann.   3.14

They then lay down to sleep, and as they lay there it was so
dark that they could not see a hand before their eyes.

Auf einmal erwachte der mit den Katzenaugen,
weckte die anderen und sprach: 3.15

Suddenly the one with the cat's eyes woke up, woke the
others and said,

3.16 »Brüder, schaut einmal auf, seht ihr die weißen Mäuschen, die da herumlaufen?«

"Brothers, look up, can you see the white little mice running around?"

3.17 Die zwei richteten sich auf, konnten aber nichts sehen.

The two sat up, but could see nothing.

3.18 Da sprach er:

Then he said,

3.19 »Es ist mit uns nicht richtig, wir haben das Unserige nicht wieder gekriegt, wir müssen zurück nach dem Wirt, der hat uns betrogen.«

"It's not right with us, we haven't got what's ours back, we have to go back to the innkeeper, he cheated us."

3.20 Also machten sie sich am anderen Morgen dahin auf und sagten dem Wirt, sie hätten ihr richtig Werk nicht wieder gekriegt, der eine hätte eine Diebeshand, der zweite Katzenaugen und der dritte ein Schweineherz.

So they set out the next morning and told the innkeeper that they had not got back what was rightly theirs, that one had a thief's hand, the second a cat's eye and the third a pig's heart.

3.21 Der Wirt sprach, daran müßte das Mädchen schuld sein und wollte es rufen, aber wie das die drei hatte kommen sehen, war es zum Hinterpförtchen fortgelaufen und kam nicht wieder.

The innkeeper said it must be the girl's fault and wanted to call her, but when she saw the three of them coming, she ran away to the back gate and did not come back.

Da sprachen die drei, er sollte ihnen viel Geld geben, 3.22
sonst ließen sie ihm den roten Hahn übers Haus
fliegen;

Then the three said he should give them a lot of money, or
they would let the red cock fly over his house;

da gab er was er hatte und nur aufbringen konnte, 3.23

so he gave what he had and could only muster,

und die drei zogen damit fort. 3.24

and the three went away with it.

Es war für ihr Lebtag genug, 3.25

It was enough for their lifetime,

sie hätten aber doch lieber ihr richtig Werk gehabt. 3.26

but they would have preferred to have their real work.

Die sieben Schwaben

The Seven Swabians

1.1 Einmal waren sieben Schwaben beisammen, der
erste war der Herr Schulz, der zweite der Jackli, der
dritte der Marli, der vierte der Jergli, der fünfte der
Michal, der sechste der Hans, der siebente der Veitli;
Once there were seven Swabians together, the first was Mr.
Schulz, the second Jackli, the third Marli, the fourth Jergli,
the fifth Michal, the sixth Hans, the seventh Veitli;

1.2 die hatten alle sieben sich vorgenommen die Welt zu
durchziehen,
all seven of them had resolved to travel the world,

1.3 Abenteuer zu suchen und große Thaten zu
vollbringen.
seek adventure and accomplish great deeds.

1.4 Damit sie aber auch mit bewaffneter Hand und sicher
gingen, sahen sie's für gut an, daß sie sich zwar nur
einen einzigen, aber recht starken und langen Spieß
machen ließen.
But in order that they might go armed and safe, they
thought it well to have only one spear made for themselves,
but a very strong and long one.

Diesen Spieß faßten sie alle sieben zusammen an, 1.5
vorn ging der kühnste und männlichste, das mußte
der Herr Schulz sein und dann folgten die anderen
nach der Reihe und der Veitli war der letzte.
All seven of them took up this spear together, the boldest
and manliest went in front, which must have been Mr.
Schulz, and then the others followed in order, with Veitli
last.

Nun geschah es, als sie im Heumonat eines Tages 2.1
einen weiten Weg gegangen waren, auch noch ein
gut Stück bis in das Dorf hatten, wo sie über Nacht
bleiben mußten, daß in der Dämmerung auf einer
Wiese ein großer Roßkäfer oder eine Hornisse nicht
weit von ihnen hinter einer Staude vorbeiflog und
feindlich brummelte.
Now it happened one day when they had gone a long way
in the month of hay, and still had a good way to go to the
village where they had to stay overnight, that at dusk in
a meadow a large horse beetle or hornet flew past not far
from them behind a shrub and buzzed hostilely.

Der Herr Schulz erschrak, daß er fast den Spieß hätte 2.2
fallen lassen und ihm der Angstschweiß am ganzen
Leibe ausbrach.
Mr. Schulz was so frightened that he almost dropped his
spear and broke out in a cold sweat all over his body.

»Horcht, horcht.« rief er seinen Gesellen, »Gott, 2.3
"Hark, hark." he called to his companions, "God,

ich höre eine Trommel!« 2.4
I hear a drum!"

2.5 Der Jackli, der hinter ihm den Spieß hielt und dem ich weiß nicht was für ein Geruch in die Nase kam, sprach:

The Jackli, who was holding the spit behind him, and whose nose was filled with I don't know what smell, said,

2.6 »Etwas ist ohne Zweifel vorhanden, denn ich schmeck das Pulver und den Zündstrick.«

"Something is there, no doubt, for I can taste the powder and the fuse."

2.7 Bei diesen Worten hob der Herr Schulz an die Flucht zu ergreifen und sprang im Hui über einen Zaun;

At these words Mr. Schulz started to flee and jumped over a fence;

2.8 weil er aber gerade auf die Zinken eines Rechen sprang, der vom Heumachen da liegen geblieben war, so fuhr ihm der Stiel ins Gesicht und gab ihm einen ungewaschenen Schlag.

but because he had just jumped on the tines of a rake that had been left there from making hay, the handle hit him in the face and gave him an unwashed blow.

2.9 »O wei, o wei.« schrie der Herr Schulz,

"Oh dear, oh dear." cried Mr. Schulz,

2.10 »nimm mich gefangen, ich ergeb mich, ich ergeb mich!«

"take me prisoner, I surrender, I surrender!"

2.11 Die anderen sechs hüpften auch alle einer über den anderen herzu und schrien:

The other six also leaped one upon the other and cried,

»Giebst du dich, so geb ich mich auch, giebst du dich,   2.12
so geb ich mich auch.«

"If you surrender, I will surrender, if you surrender, I will
surrender."

Endlich, wie kein Feind da war, der sie binden und   2.13
fortführen wollte, merkten sie, daß sie betrogen
waren;

At last, as there was no enemy to bind them and lead them
away, they realized that they had been deceived;

und damit die Geschichte nicht unter die Leute   2.14
käme, und sie nicht genarrt und gespottet würden,
verschwuren sie sich untereinander, solange davon
stillzuschweigen, bis einer unverhofft das Maul
aufthäte.

and lest the story should get out among the people, and
they should be fooled and ridiculed, they conspired among
themselves to keep silence about it until one of them should
unexpectedly open his mouth.

Hierauf zogen sie weiter.   3.1

They then moved on.

Die zweite Gefährlichkeit, die sie erlebten, kann aber   3.2
mit der ersten nicht verglichen werden.

The second peril they experienced, however, cannot be
compared with the first.

Nach etlichen Tagen trug sie ihr Weg durch ein   3.3
Brachfeld, da saß ein Hase in der Sonne und schlief,
streckte die Ohren in die Höhe, und hatte die großen
gläsernen Augen starr aufstehen.

After several days, their path took them through a fallow
field, where a hare was sitting in the sun and sleeping, its
ears stretched upwards and its large glassy eyes fixed.

3.4 Da erschraken sie bei dem Anblick des grausamen und wilden Tieres insgesamt und hielten Rat,

They were frightened at the sight of the ferocious and wild animal,

3.5 was zu thun das wenigst gefährliche wäre.

and took counsel as to what would be the least dangerous thing to do.

3.6 Denn so sie fliehen wollten, war zu besorgen, das Ungeheuer setzte ihnen nach und verschlänge sie alle mit Haut und Haar.

For if they wanted to flee, it was to be feared that the monster would chase after them and devour them all with skin and hair.

3.7 Also sprachen sie:

So they said:

3.8 »Wir müssen einen große und gefährlichen Kampf bestehen,

"We must fight a great and dangerous battle,

3.9 frisch gewagt ist halb gewonnen!«

freshly ventured is half won!"

3.10 faßten alle sieben den Spieß an,

All seven took up the spear,

3.11 der Herr Schulz vorn und der Veitli hinten.

Mr. Schulz in front and Veitli behind.

Der Herr Schulz wollte den Spieß noch immer anhalten, der Veitli aber war hinten ganz mutig geworden, wollte losbrechen und rief: 3.12

Mr. Schulz still wanted to hold the spear, but Mr. Veitli had become quite courageous at the back, wanted to break loose and shouted:

»Stoß zu in aller Schwabe Name,

"Shove in all Swabian name,

sonst wünsch i, daß Ihr möcht erlahme.«

otherwise I wish that you may fall asleep."

Aber der Hans wußte ihn zu treffen und sprach: 5.1

But Hans knew how to meet him and spoke:

»Beim Element, du hascht gut schwätze,

"By the element, you're a good talker,

bischt stets der letscht beim Drachehetze.«

is always the last one at the dragon hunt."

Der Michael rief: 7.1

Michael called out:

»Es wird nit fehle um ein Haar,

"It won't miss by a hair,

so ischt es wohl der Teufel gar.«

it is probably the devil himself."

Drauf kam an den Jergli die Reihe, der sprach: 9.1

Then it was Jergli's turn to speak:

»Ischt er es nit, so ischt's sei Muter,

"If it's not him, it's his mother,

oder des Teufels Stiefbruder.«

or the devil's stepbrother."

11.1 Der Marli hatte da einen guten Gedanken und sagte zum Veitli:

Marli had a good idea and said to Veitli:

»Gang, Veitli, gang, gang du voran,

"Go, Veitli, go, go ahead,

i will dahinte vor di stahn.«

I want to stand there in front of you."

13.1 Der Veitli hörte aber nicht darauf und der Jackli sagt:

But Veitli didn't listen and Jackli said:

»Der Schulz, der muß der erschte sei,

"Schulz, he must be the first,

denn ihm gebührt die Ehr allei.«

for to him all honor is due."

15.1 Da nahm sich der Herr Schulz ein Herz und sprach gravitätisch:

Then Mr. Schulz took heart and spoke gravely:

»So zieht denn herzhaft in den Streit,

"So enter the fray with all your heart,

hieran erkennt man tapfre Leut.«

This is how you recognize brave people."

Da gingen sie insgesamt auf den Drachen los.   17.1

Then they all went after the dragon.

Der Herr Schulz segnete sich und rief Gott um   17.2
Beistand an; wie aber alles nicht helfen wollte und
er dem Feind immer näher kam, schrie er in großer
Angst:

Mr. Schulz blessed himself and called on God for help, but
as nothing helped and he came closer and closer to the
enemy, he shouted in great fear:

»Hau! hurehau! hau! hauhau!« Davon erwachte der   17.3
Hase,

"Hau! hurehau! hau! hauhau!" The hare woke up,

erschrak und sprang eilig davon.   17.4

was frightened and jumped away in a hurry.

Als ihn der Herr Schulz so feldflüchtig sah,   17.5

When Mr. Schulz saw him fleeing from the field,

da rief er voll Freude: 17.6

he shouted with joy:

»Potz, Veitli, lueg, lueg, was   "Potz, Veitli, lueg, lueg,
isch das?   what's that?

das Ungehüer ischt a Has.«   the monster is a hare."

19.1 Der Schwabenbund suchte aber weiter Abenteuer
und kam an die Mosel, ein mosiges, stilles und tiefes
Wasser, darüber nicht viel Brücken sind, sondern
man an mehreren Orten sich muß in Schiffen
überfahren lassen.

But the Swabian League went on in search of adventure
and came to the Moselle, a mossy, still and deep water, over
which there are not many bridges, but in several places you
have to cross in boats.

19.2 Weil die sieben Schwaben dessen unberichtet waren,
riefen sie einem Mann, der jenseits des Wassers
seine Arbeit vollbrachte, zu, wie man doch hinüber
kommen Könnte? Der Mann verstand wegen der
Weite und wegen ihrer Sprache nicht was sie wollten,
und fragte auf sein Trierisch: »Wat? wat?« Da meinte
der Herr Schulz, er spräche nicht anders als: »Wate,
wate durchs Wasser.«

As the seven Swabians were unaware of this, they called out
to a man who was working on the other side of the water,
asking how they could get across.«

19.3 und hob an, weil er der vorderste war, sich auf den
Weg zu machen und in die Mosel hineinzugehen.

The man didn't understand what they wanted because of
the distance and their language, and asked in his native
Trierese: "Wat? wat?" Then Mr. Schulz said that he could
only say: "Wate, wate through the water" and, because he
was the foremost, he set off and entered the Moselle.

19.4 Nicht lange, so versank sank er in den Schlamm und
in die antreibenden tiefen Wellen, seinen Hut aber
jagte der Wind hinüber an das jenseitige Ufer, und
ein Frosch setzte sich dabei und quakte:

Before long, he sank into the mud and the driving deep
waves, but the wind blew his hat over to the far bank, and a
frog sat down and croaked:

»Wat, wat, wat.«   19.5
"Wat, wat, wat."

Die sechs anderen hörten das drüben und sprachen: 19.6
The six others heard this and said:

»Unser Gesell, der Herr Schulz, ruft uns, kann er   19.7
hinüber waten, warum wir nicht auch?«
"Our companion, Mr. Schulz, is calling us, can he wade
across, why don't we?"

Sprangen darum eilig alle zusammen in das   19.8
Wasser und ertranken, also, daß ein Frosch ihrer
sechse ums Leben brachte, und niemand von dem
Schwabenbund wieder nach Hause kam.
So they all jumped into the water together in a hurry and
drowned, so that a frog killed the six of them, and none of
the Swabians came home again.

Die drei Handwerksburschen
The Three Craftsmen

1.1 Es waren drei Handwerksburschen, die hatten es verabredet, auf ihrer Wanderung beisammen zu bleiben und immer in einer Stadt zu arbeiten.
There were three craftsmen who had agreed to stay together on their journey and always work in one town.

1.2 Auf eine Zeit aber fanden sie bei ihren Meister kein Verdienst mehr, sodaß sie endlich ganz abgerissen waren und nichts zu leben hatten.
After a time, however, they found that they could no longer earn any money from their masters, so that at last they were completely torn up and had nothing to live on.

1.3 Da sprach der eine: »Was sollen wir anfangen?
Then one of them said, "What shall we do?

Hier bleiben können wir nicht länger, wir wollen 1.4
wieder wandern, und wenn wir in der Stadt, wo
wir hinkommen, keine Arbeit finden, so wollen
wir beim Herbergsvater ausmachen, daß wir ihm
schreiben, wo wir uns aufhalten, und einer vom
anderen Nachricht haben kann, und dann wollen wir
uns trennen.«

We can stay here no longer, we want to wander again, and
if we cannot find work in the town where we are going, we
will arrange with the innkeeper that we will write to him
where we are staying, so that one of us may have news of
the other, and then we will part."

das schien den anderen auch das beste. 1.5

That seemed the best thing to the others.

Sie zogen fort, da kam ihnen auf dem Wege ein 1.6
reichgekleideter Mann entgegen, der fragte, wer
sie wären.

They set off, and on the way a richly dressed man met them
and asked who they were.

»Wir sind Handwerksleute und suchen Arbeit; 1.7

"We are craftsmen and are looking for work;

wir haben uns bisher zusammengehalten, wenn wir 1.8
aber keine mehr finden, so wollen wir uns trennen.«

we have stuck together until now, but if we can't find any
more, we want to split up."

»Das hat keine Not.« sprach der Mann, 1.9

"There is no need of that." said the man,

»wenn ihr thun wollt, was ich euch sage, soll's euch 1.10
an Geld und Arbeit nicht fehlen;

"if you will do as I tell you, you shall not want for money
and work;

1.11 ja, ihr sollt große Herren werden und in Kutschen fahren.«

yes, you shall become great masters and ride in carriages."

1.12 Der eine sprach,

The one said,

1.13 »Wenn's unserer Seele und Seligkeit nicht schadet,

"If it does not harm our souls and happiness,

1.14 so wollen wir's wohl thun.«

we will do it."

1.15 »Nein.« antwortete der Mann,

"No." answered the man,

1.16 »ich Habe keinen Teil an euch.«

"I have no part in you."

1.17 Der andere aber hatte nach seinen Füßen gesehen, und als er da einen Pferdefuß und einen Menschenfuß erblickte, wollte er sich nicht mit ihm einlassen.

The other, however, had looked at his feet, and when he saw a horse's foot and a man's foot, he did not want to get involved with him.

1.18 Der Teufel aber sprach:

But the devil said,

1.19 »Gebt euch zufrieden, es ist nicht auf euch abgesehen, sondern auf eines anderen Seele, der schon halb mein ist und dessen Maß nur voll laufen soll.«

"Be content, it is not you who are after, but another soul, who is already half mine and whose measure is only to run full."

Weil sie nun sicher waren, willigten sie ein, und der Teufel sagte ihnen, was er verlangte: 1.20

Now that they were sure, they agreed, and the devil told them what he wanted:

der erste sollte auf jede Frage antworten: »Wir alle drei.« 1.21

the first was to answer every question: "All three of us."

der zweite »um's Geld.« der dritte »und das war recht.« 1.22

the second "for the money." the third "and that was right."

Das sollten sie immer hintereinander sagen, weiter aber dürften sie kein Wort sprechen, und überträten sie das Gebot, so wäre gleich alles Geld verschwunden; 1.23

They were to say this one after the other, but they were not allowed to say anything else, and if they broke the commandment, all the money would be gone immediately;

solange sie es aber befolgten, 1.24

but as long as they obeyed it,

sollten ihre Taschen immer voll sein. 1.25

their pockets would always be full.

Zum Anfang gab er ihnen auch gleich so viel als sie tragen konnten und hieß sie in die Stadt in das und das Wirtshaus gehen. 1.26

To begin with, he gave them as much as they could carry and told them to go into town to the inn.

Sie gingen hinein, der Wirt kam ihnen entgegen und fragte: 1.27

They went in, the innkeeper met them and asked:

1.28 »Wollt ihr etwas essen?« Der erste antwortete:
"Do you want something to eat?" The first replied:

1.29 »Wir alle drei.«
"All three of us."

1.30 »Ja.« sagte der Wirt, »das mein ich auch.«
"Yes." said the innkeeper, "that's what I mean."

1.31 Der zweite: »Ums Geld.«
The second: "For the money."

1.32 »Das versteht sich.« sagte der Wirt. Der dritte:
"That goes without saying." said the innkeeper. The third:

1.33 »Und das war recht.«
"And that was right."

1.34 »Jawohl, war's recht.« sagte der, Wirt.
"Yes, it was right." said the innkeeper.

1.35 Es ward ihnen nun gut Essen und Trinken gebracht und wohl aufgewartet.
They were now brought good food and drink and well waited on.

1.36 Nach dem Essen mußte die Bezahlung geschehen, da hielt der Wirt dem einen die Rechnung hin, der sprach:
After the meal they had to pay, and the innkeeper held out the bill to one of them, who said:

1.37 »Wir alle drei.« der zweite: »ums Geld.«
"All three of us." The second: "For the money."

1.38 der dritte: »und das war recht.«
The third: "And that was right."

»Freilich ist's recht.« sagte der Wirt,   1.39
"Of course it's right." said the innkeeper,

»alle drei bezahlen, und ohne Geld kann ich nichts   1.40
geben.«
"all three pay, and without money I can't give anything."

Sie bezahlten aber noch mehr als er gefordert hatte.   1.41
But they paid even more than he had asked for.

Die Gäste sahen das mit an und sprachen,   1.42
The guests saw this and said,

»Die Leute müssen toll sein.«   1.43
"These people must be great."

»Ja, das sind sie auch.« sagte der Wirt,   1.44
"Yes, they are." said the innkeeper,

»sie sind nicht recht klug.«   1.45
"they're not very clever."

So blieben sie eine Zeitlang in dem Wirtshaus und   1.46
sprachen kein ander Wort als:
So they stayed in the inn for a while and said nothing but:

»Wir alle drei, ums Geld, und das war recht.«   1.47
"All three of us, for the money, and that was right."

Sie sahen aber und wußten alles was darin vorging.   1.48
But they saw and knew all that was going on.

Es trug sich zu, daß ein großer Kaufmann kam mit   1.49
vielem Geld, Her sprach:
It happened that a great merchant came with a great deal of
money, and said,

1.50 »Herr Wirt, heb Er mir mein Geld auf, da sind die drei närrischen Handwerksburschen, die möchten mir's stehlen.«

"Sir innkeeper, save my money, there are three foolish tradesmen who want to steal it from me."

1.51 Das that der Wirt.

So the innkeeper did.

1.52 Wie er den Mantelsack in seine Stube trug, fühlte er, daß er schwer von Gold war.

As he carried the cloak-bag into his parlor, he felt that it was heavy with gold.

1.53 Darauf gab er den drei Handwerkern unten ein Lager,

Then he gave the three workmen a place to sleep downstairs,

1.54 der Kaufmann aber kam oben hin in eine besondere Stube.

but the merchant went upstairs to a special room.

1.55 Als Mitternacht war und der Wirt dachte, sie schliefen alle, kam er mit seiner Frau, und sie hatten eine Holzaxt und schlugen den reichen Kaufmann tot;

When it was midnight, and the innkeeper thought they were all asleep, he came with his wife, and they had a wooden axe, and beat the rich merchant to death;

1.56 nach vollbrachtem Mord legten sie sich, wieder schlafen.

after the murder was done, they lay down to sleep again.

Wie's nun Tag' war, gab's großen Lärm, der
Kaufmann lag tot im Bett und schwamm in seinem
Blut.

As it was now day, there was a great noise, the merchant lay
dead in bed, swimming in his blood.

1.57

Da liefen alle Gäste zusammen, der Wirt aber sprach,

Then all the guests ran together, but the innkeeper said,

1.58

»Das haben die drei tollen Handwerker gethan.«

"The three mad craftsmen did this."

1.59

Die Gäste bestätigten, es und sagten:

The guests confirmed it and said:

1.60

»Niemand anders kann's gewesen sein.«

"It couldn't have been anyone else."

1.61

Der Wirt aber ließ sie rufen und sagte zu ihnen,

But the innkeeper called them and said to them,

1.62

»Habt ihr den Kaufmann getötet?«

"Did you kill the merchant?"

1.63

»Wir alle drei.« sagte der erste, »ums Geld.«

"All three of us." said the first, "for money."

1.64

der zweite, »und das war recht« der dritte.

said the second, "and that was right" said the third.

1.65

Da hört ihr's nun.« sprach der Wirt,

Now you hear it." said the innkeeper,

1.66

»sie gestehen's selber.«

"they confess it themselves."

1.67

1.68 Sie wurden also ins Gefängnis gebracht und sollten gerichtet werden.

So they were taken to prison and were to be judged.

1.69 Wie sie nun sahen, daß es so ernsthaft ging, ward ihnen doch angst, aber nachts kam der Teufel und sprach:

When they saw that things were going so seriously, they were afraid, but at night the devil came and said,

1.70 »Haltet nur noch einen Tag aus, und verscherzt euer Glück nicht, es soll euch kein Haar gekrümmt werden.«

"Hold out just one more day, and don't spoil your luck, not a hair of your head shall be harmed."

1.71 Am anderen Morgen wurden sie vor Gericht geführt,

The next morning,

1.72 da sprach der Richter:

they were brought to court and the judge said:

1.73 »Seid ihr die Mörder?«

"Are you the murderers?"

1.74 »Wir alle drei.«

"All three of us."

1.75 »Warum habt ihr den Kaufmann erschlagen?«

"Why did you kill the merchant?"

1.76 »Ums Geld.«

"For the money."

1.77 »Ihr Bösewichter.« sagte der Richter,

"You villains." said the judge,

»habt ihr euch nicht der Sünde gescheut?«

1.78

"did you not shy away from sin?"

»Und das war recht.«

1.79

"And that was right."

»Sie haben bekannt und sind, noch halsstarrig dazu.«

1.80

"You have confessed, and are stiff-necked to boot."

sprach der Richter, »führt sie gleich zum Tode.«

1.81

said the judge, "lead them straight to death."

Also wurden sie hinausgebracht,

1.82

So they were taken out,

und der Wirt mußte mit in den Kreis treten.

1.83

and the innkeeper had to join them in the circle.

Wie sie nun von den Henkersknechten gefaßt
und oben aufs Gerüst geführt wurden, wo der
Scharfrichter mit bloßem Schwerte stand, kam auf
einmal eine Kutsche mit vier blutroten Füchsen
bespannt und fuhr, daß das Feuer aus den Steinen
sprangt aus dem Fenster aber winkte einer mit einem
weißen Tuche.

1.84

As they were seized by the executioner's servants and led
to the top of the scaffold, where the executioner stood
with his bare sword, a carriage with four blood-red foxes
suddenly came and drove along, so that the fire leaped out
of the stones, but from the window one of them waved a
white scarf.

Da sprach der Scharfrichter: »Es kommt Gnade.«

1.85

Then the executioner said, "Mercy is coming."

und ward aus dem Wagen »Gnade! Gnade!« gerufen.

1.86

and "Mercy! Mercy!" was shouted.

1.87 Da trat der Teufel heraus, als ein sehr vornehmer
Herr, prächtig gekleidet und sprach,
Then the devil came out as a very distinguished gentleman,
splendidly dressed, and said,

1.88 »Ihr drei seid unschuldig;
"You three are innocent;

1.89 ihr dürft nun sprechen, sagt heraus, was ihr gesehen
und gehört habt.«
you may now speak, tell us what you have seen and heard."

1.90 Da sprach der älteste: »Wir haben den Kaufmann
nicht getötet,
Then the eldest said, "We did not kill the merchant,

1.91 der Mörder steht da im Kreise.«
the murderer is standing there in the circle."

1.92 und deutete auf den Wirt,
and pointed to the innkeeper,

1.93 »zum Wahrzeichen geht hin in seinen Keller,
da hängen noch viele andere, die er ums Leben
gebracht.«
"go to his cellar as a symbol, there are many others hanging
there whom he has killed."

1.94 Da schickte der Richter die Henkersknechte hin, die
fanden es, wie's gesagt war, und als sie dem Richter
das berichtet hatten, ließ er den Wirt hinaufführen
und ihm das Haupt abschlagen.
Then the judge sent the executioner's servants, who found
it as it was said, and when they had reported it to the judge,
he had the innkeeper brought up and his head cut off.

1.95 Da sprach der Teufel zu den dreien:
Then the devil said to the three:

»Nun hab' ich die Seele, die ich haben wollte, ihr seid aber frei und habt Geld für euer Lebtag.«

1.96

"Now I have the soul I wanted, but you are free and have money for life."

Möwenstein Books

www.mowenstein.com

Renowned Authors

H. G. Wells · Ernest Hemingway
H. P. Lovecraft · Lewis Carroll
Franz Kafka · Friedrich Nietzsche
Albert Einstein · Oscar Wilde
Hans Christian Andersen

Notable Works

Frankenstein · *Alice in Wonderland*
Heart of Darkness · *The Great Gatsby*
Siddhartha · *The Metamorphosis*
Thus Spoke Zarathustra

Translation Services

We offer translation services in various languages, including German, Spanish, Chinese, Korean, Arabic, and more. For custom translations or revisions, please contact us at:

Email: translation@mowenstein.com

Our Collections

Franz Kafka Collection

- The Metamorphosis / Die Verwandlung
- The Trial / Der Prozess
- The Castle / Das Schloss
- and many more...

Pakt mit dem Teufel

- Faust Parts I & II by Johann Wolfgang von Goethe
- Doctor Faustus by Christopher Marlowe

Portraits of Irishmen

- The Picture of Dorian Gray by Oscar Wilde
- A Portrait of the Artist as a Young Man by James Joyce

Children's Classics

- Winnie-the-Pooh / Pu der Bär
- Brothers Grimm Fairy Tales
- Fairy Tales Told for Children
    - Author: Hans Christian Andersen

Visit Us

At Möwenstein Books, we are committed to providing high-quality bilingual editions of classic works. Explore our collections and discover more titles across various genres and languages.

Website: www.mowenstein.com